Creation Salvation & End Times

Creation Salvation & End Times

A Bible Scholar Answers
70 Questions in 121 Pages

ALLEN LINN

Copyright © 2020 by Allen Linn

Minneapolis, Minnesota
patrickday@pyramidpublishers.com

All rights reserved. No part of this publication may be reproduced, stored in a retrieval system, or transmitted, in any form or by any means, electronic, mechanical, photocopying, recording, or otherwise, without the prior written permission of the author.

Printed by Lightning Source
1246 Heil Quaker Blvd.
La Vergne, TN USA 37086
ISBN – 978-0-9982014-9-8

Cover Design by Van-garde Imagery, Inc.
Interior Layout by Van-garde Imagery, Inc.
Printed in the United States of America

Unless otherwise noted, Scripture quotations are from The Holy Bible, New International Version™, NIV™, Copyright © 1973, 1978, 1984, 2011 by Biblica, Inc.™ Used by permission of Zondervan

Introduction

I was saved at the age of 17 and found myself struggling with the Bible at first. It didn't take me long to realize I was dealing with God's revelation, but what that revelation was I didn't know. One day I heard a minister say, "Jesus is the answer." A man next to me turned and said mockingly, "If Jesus is the answer, what is the question?" I never forgot what that man said.

As I continued to wrestle with the Scriptures, it soon dawned on me that the questions Jesus was the answer to were simply these: "What is the meaning of existence? Why are we here? Is there a purpose to our existence?"

Once God enabled me to grasp this, I realized He was driving me to search the Scriptures. After more than 50 years, I still have that same drive. Over the years, many people have asked me questions about the Bible. Some were asked in mockery, but most were asked with honest hearts and a desire to know the deeper issues of life. This book contains the answers to many of these questions.

Table of Contents

1. Creation 9
2. Salvation 19
3. End Times 53
4. Questions About the Bible 81
5. Constantine 121
6. George Washington 125
7. Abraham Lincoln 127

1. Creation

What is the main argument against evolution and what is the main argument for Biblical Creation?
There are many arguments against the theory of evolution but these are not well known because evolution is a protected philosophy. Certainly, one of the biggest arguments against the theory of evolution is the fossil record, because if evolution did take place it would have to be documented by fossils.

If evolution took place over millions of years from very simple species to more and more complex forms, a very large number of intermediary stages would have arisen and this would be evident with fossils. This was crucial to Darwin's theory. If life evolved on earth, the fossil record would begin with very simple life forms in the oldest rocks on the bottom layer. From there we would expect to find very small transitions from simple to more complex life forms.

It would be one continual record of gradually changing creatures. They would all have distinct features of gradual change. First would be the one creature and then another creature that evolved from the first. There would be no definite gaps in the record between species as there are now. In fact, there would be no definite species but all would be evolving into a different kind of species.

Imagine marine invertebrates evolving into fish and then evolving into amphibians and then into reptiles, which would then evolve into apes and finally into man. And yet marine invertebrate, fish, amphibians and reptiles and apes are still living with mankind. They have not given way to an advanced species.

Darwin was troubled by the lack of intermediate links connecting one species to another in the fossil record and wrote: "Intermediate links? Geology assuredly does not reveal any such finely graduated organic change. And this is perhaps the most obvious and serious objection which can be urged against the theory."

He later wrote: "The number of intermediate links between the living and extinct species must have been inconceivably great."

Since then, we now have billions of fossils of each species represented by cataloged fossils taken from every one of the geologic periods. Imagine the tremendous number of intermediary stages we should have in the fossil record if, as evolutionists teach, the species have gradually evolved during the hundreds of millions of years of evolution. We should have millions of these intermediary fossils. How many in fact do we have? Exactly none!

If evolution is true, there should be no distinct species. All life forms should be evolving transitional forms, since all species would be evolving into other species, since evolutionary change is supposedly the basic law of nature.

The very earliest fossil records, which supposedly appear about 600 million years ago, should be in the oldest rocks. These rocks contain so many fossils that the period is called the *Cambrian Explosion*. These creatures are supposedly the first examples of real life.

Here we should find the simplest forms of life that eventually evolved into the more and more complex creatures of today. However, the animals found there are the same as today. They appear suddenly and fully developed, with no trace of evolutionary development from the single-cell life forms into complex vertebrates. How could this happen over a period of more than two billion years without leaving a single fossil? There are absolutely no traces of intermediate stages.

Not a single intermediary fossil has ever been found and there should be literally millions of them. The various species were fixed from the beginning. The theory of evolution is a desperate attempt to push God out of His own creation in order to avoid accountability to an Almighty God. It is the foolish attempt of fallen mankind to pretend the nonexistence of the very One who gives life meaning and purpose.

What is the main argument for Biblical Creation?
The following is taken from my book, *The Bible Explained*.

The ancient myths of creation all begin with matter in some form or another, as do the so-called more sophisticated theories of evolution. They all begin with space, matter and time. Only the Bible begins with the First Cause: an Eternal, Almighty, and Personal God. Only this can explain the intelligent design of creation with life and personality.

Biblical creation begins with God alone. He was the preexisting intelligence and power necessary to bring creation into being, operating from another dimension. God created everything out of nothing. He simply spoke the creation into existence.

The universe is clearly a place of thought and planning. Only persons can think and plan. If you find yourself in a room with a soda machine, you put your money in and the machine gives you a soda. We know that matter cannot think. A person who can think had to design that machine to obey a certain built-in response to the money being inserted.

Machines do not think; matter does not think. The stars and planets and other material bodies did not get together and decide which laws they would obey and operate under. A Great Designer did this. As a house is not built simply to look at, while walking through it, one realizes that it was built for people. So also, the earth was created for people. As one scientist has said: "It's as though the universe knew we were coming."

Where Does Sin Come From?

The following is taken from my two books, *The Bible Explained* and *Battling Spiritual Warfare*.

Perhaps the most vexing question confronting a thinking person is: If God is a loving God why is there evil and suffering in the world? The answer from Scripture is that these came into the world through man's sin.

The next question is: If God knew this would happen, why did He allow it? All the suffering and death in the world that God created to be *very good* could have been avoided if God had not allowed sin into His perfect creation. This is true, but mankind was created to be a morally responsible being and this is only possible if man has the freedom to choose.

God is never the cause of sin, but He does allow His creatures freedom to choose sin; then He directs and controls it for good. Sin comes from our ability to do the opposite of what God wants. Mankind does not have to wonder what might have happened if God had allowed us to choose our own way. Now we know. But even after we choose our own wills over God's will, God allows us to use our freedom to come back to Him, through Christ's sacrifice on our behalf.

Lucifer's fall occurred shortly before mankind's creation. He renounced his allegiance to the Most High and became the leader of an unnumbered host of fallen angels called demons. When God threw Lucifer and his followers out of heaven to earth for their rebellion, he became known as Satan. He is referred to in the Bible as the "ruler of this present age of darkness," and the leader of "the spiritual hosts of wickedness in the heavenly realms," an organized hierarchy of fallen angels.

He became the great adversary of God and His people. From that time on, there has been a great division in the cosmos as an opposing kingdom of darkness was born to challenge the universal kingdom of God. God allowed this to happen for His own purpose. He would allow the devil to have his way within the limits of God's overruling will. God allows these things to take place for our good.

It would teach us the consequences of going our own way. We were created for the highest purpose possible – to enjoy a loving relationship with our Creator. God did not create us as mere puppets that He could simply pull a string on our backs for a programmed response of love. True love must be chosen not forced. God loves us with a sincere and genuine love and he wants this love in return.

It would allow God to reveal the depth of His love for His fallen creation and allow mankind freedom to choose Him or reject Him. Mankind was created with freedom of choice. But this freedom had to be exercised by giving him a choice. Mankind was created for a relationship of love, but love must be chosen freely. A mere robot cannot truly love its Maker.

Mankind was given dominion over the whole creation. The center of his rule was a beautiful garden. Mankind was created for intimate fellowship with God, and the garden is where God met with them. God wanted a relationship of love, and love must be chosen freely.

They could eat of every tree with only one exception. The tree of the "knowledge of good and evil," so-called because *good* would result if they obeyed and *evil* if they did not. Eating the forbidden fruit would give experiential knowledge of good and evil (Genesis 2:9).

Lucifer, now called Satan, was allowed to tempt them. They chose to follow Satan and ate the forbidden fruit. At this point, they had taken control of their own lives, and they had made themselves their own masters. Now, instead of God, they would write the unwritten history of the human race. Their own individual wills had replaced the will of God. Satan had driven a wedge between God and humanity.

The apostle Paul summed it up thusly: "Therefore, just as sin entered the world through one man, and death came through sin, and in this way death came to all men, because all sinned" (Romans 5:12). As the Representative Man, when Adam sinned, sin entered the world and spread to everyone. For in Adam we all sinned. Adam's sinful nature was passed to all men and leads to the practice of sin.

All creation was put under the curse and death spread to everyone: "Against its will, all creation was subjected to God's curse" (Romans 8:20). Life became a struggle filled with grief and suffering in the world. God would remove His hand and allow creation to move toward disorder and death. Man's whole environment was under the curse, confronting him with the tragedy of sin and his inability to reverse his journey toward death and judgment.

Mankind would have to fill his time with labor just to live. Creation was now in conflict with them. Their dominion was now one of cruelty, pain, suffering and hardship. The universe came under the universal law of decay and death. All things that were made are being unmade – aging, wearing out, and finally dying. Disappointment and futility dominate the cosmos.

They would return to dust physically and face judgment. The world that God had filled with life was now filled with death. Satan became the "Prince of this world" (John 12:31; 14:30) and the "god of this age [mindset]" (2 Corinthians 4:4).

Instead of exalting God as the center of his universe, mankind took the position of everything revolving around himself. This is sin in its essence. Yet because man is born a sinner, he is unaware that he is one. He ascends the throne of his own life and declares: "I am God!"

However, God has set a day when it will be said: "The whole world has now become the kingdom of our Lord and of His Christ, and He will reign forever and ever" (Revelation 11:15). "Then I heard what sounded like a great multitude, like the roar of rushing waters, and like loud pearls of thunder, shouting, Hallelujah! For our Lord God reigns" (Revelation 19:6).

But until then, the earth stands under the shadow of death. Life will be a gradual dying, and birth will be the beginning of death.

Is God the author of sin? Please explain God's sovereignty and man's free will. What does the Bible say? How can the world God created be sinful, and then He condemns us when we sin? It makes me think God is cruel to create men and women who sin and then smash them when they do.

No, God is not the Author of sin. Yes, God is sovereign but yet man has free will.

God is sovereign while granting mankind free will. While God could dictate all human events that will take place, He chooses not to. The reason for this should be obvious. God did not create mankind as robots but as free individuals who can choose whether to love God or not and whether to obey Him or not. God's sovereignty means that God can do whatever He wants to. He is all-powerful, all-knowing, and His purposes cannot be overcome.

However, God is also love, and His purpose is that mankind has free will to love Him or reject Him. To say that God's sovereignty means that whatever happens is God's will make God a partaker of our sins, and this is impossible. Why? Because God's holiness prevents this. God cannot go against His own nature.

God's nature is love, and the love He wants in return is genuine, not like an action figure whose string He pulls and the figure says, "I love you, Daddy." Mankind's freedom is necessary for the real love that God wants. And while giving us genuine freedom to love Him, He must allow us not to love Him. To truly be able to respond to His love, we must be able to not respond to His love.

Love that is forced is not truly love. Love can only be voluntary, not forced. God does not break our stubborn will by sheer raw power but by love. Mankind has free choice, and God has not surrendered His sovereignty. His sovereign plan takes into account our fee will.

Some teach that if mankind has to choose to believe (rather than being sovereignly forced to believe), then he is contributing to his own salvation. But that's like saying that if a man gives a beggar money and the beggar holds out his hand to receive the free gift, that the beggar earned the money.

There is no merit in believing in Christ. Believing in Christ is simply the hand that receives the free gift from God. Christ went to the cross to purchase our salvation, for which He gets all the glory, but which we are responsible to receive.

2. Salvation

Would you please explain unconditional election?
Unconditional election is the teaching of Calvinism, based upon *Total Depravity* and *Unconditional Election*, the first two letters of the acronym T.U.L.I.P. This is a misinterpretation of God's sovereignty and is the foundation of Calvinism.

The dogma of Calvinism explains that every thought, word, and action of mankind is decreed by God – this includes all sin. This would mean that mankind does not have free will as the Scriptures declare he has. Without free will, mankind is a mere robot.

According to Calvinism, it follows that if God is sovereign then mankind cannot have free will. But one must ask what kind of sovereignty is it that cannot allow mankind free will? The Bible is emphatic that mankind was created for a love relationship with God, and this is not possible without free will.

Based upon Calvinism's view of grace, man's faith and response to God's offer of salvation is considered a work, whereas God's election must be unconditional.

According to Calvinism, if election is based upon something man does, such as repentance and faith in Christ, then God's grace is compromised. God must intervene sovereignly to regenerate the elect without faith in Christ. It is by God's sovereign regeneration that God sovereignly produces faith.

Furthermore, if a person has to accept a gift, it would be the same as earning it. Even faith is considered a work. But the Scriptures contrast faith and works. "For it is by grace you have been saved through faith – and this is not from yourselves, it is the gift of God – not by works, so that no one can boast" (Ephesians 2:8-9).

How are we saved according to Scripture? Is it unconditional? The means of salvation is grace based upon what Christ did in our behalf: "For it is by grace you have been saved." How do we receive this grace? "Through faith – not by works."

Calvinists say that to reject unconditional election is to reject salvation by grace and promote salvation by works.

To support Calvinism, Scripture must be disputed in many places and word meanings distorted and changed. Suppose a man who has a loving family goes to bed at night and wakes up in the morning to find that his wife and kids only loved him because they were programmed to do so with a little disk implanted in their brains. Would he be disappointed? Of course, he would be.

He would be disappointed because true love must be freely given not artificially implanted in the brain. God did not take upon Himself humanity and suffer and die an agonizing death in order to have a bunch of robots tell him how much they love Him. God created human beings in His own image so they could freely and willingly love Him. Human beings without free will are not human beings but robots.

The Bible clearly teaches that God is omniscient, that He knows all before it happens. This is foreknowledge of all events before they happen. Calvinism limits God's foreknowledge by teaching that God knows only what He has decreed. And for God to be omniscient and know all, He must be the cause of everything that happens, including all evil. As Arthur Pink mistakenly states: "Not only did His omniscient eye see Adam eating of the forbidden fruit, but He decreed beforehand that He should do so" (*The Sovereignty of God*, page 249). The doctrine of unconditional election naturally follows.

But God does not have to decree all events in order to be omniscient. God, being in another dimension, is separate from His creation and sees it from outside of time. For God, there is no time, no past or future to Him, but He sees all things from the present perspective.

If mankind's rebellion and fall were simply the carrying out of what God had decreed He must do, this would make God the author of sin and mankind mere puppets. If God decreed mankind to sin and disobey, how can it be called disobedience to do what He has ordained us to do?

I believe Calvinists do not see the full meaning of what they are saying about God's character – that He would foreordain mankind to sin and then punish them for what He had caused them to do. He would be damning them before bringing them into existence.

Calvinists enhance words to support their theology. For instance, the word *world* seems obviously to refer to everyone, but the Calvinists say it means only the elect. *Any*, in turn, means any among the elect; *whosoever* means whosoever among the elect.

When the Scriptures say, "Christ Jesus came into the world to save sinners" (I Timothy 1:15), it would mean the elect among sinners. These enhancements are necessary because otherwise, some passages of Scripture would not support Calvinism. Take John 3:16 as an example of what happens without redefining *world* and *whosoever* – "God so loved the world (the world of mankind), that He gave His one and only Son, that whosoever (among the world of mankind) believes in Him shall not perish but have eternal life."

Calvinists say that election is unconditional and a mystery of God's hidden will. But the Scriptures say that God does have a reason for choosing His elect: "Who have been chosen according to the foreknowledge of God the Father" (I Peter 1:2). Election and predestination are based on God's foreknowledge of those who will believe in Christ.

The following is taken from my book, *The Bible Explained*:

> God's sovereignty is clearly taught in the Scriptures, as is His love. Within the divine nature, there can be no conflict in His attributes. All His actions are in perfect union. He cannot divide Himself and act according to one attribute while the others remain inactive. These attributes describe God's very nature. They simply describe God as being Himself.

God created mankind for the purpose of a love relationship. Love must be chosen freely, not forced. This required mankind to have free will. Calvinism over-emphasizes God's sovereignty at the expense of His love. God's desire that all mankind be saved (2 Peter 3:9) is genuine, but so is His desire that His love be freely accepted. So no one really is unconditionally elected. Mankind's acceptance or rejection is based upon their acceptance or rejection of God's ultimate act of love, the giving of the greatest gift that God can give – His one and only Son, Jesus Christ.

Those who receive Christ do not feel like they earned their salvation by believing. They glory in Christ alone who took our place in judgment and paid the penalty for our sins. And those who reject Christ cannot blame God for not electing them. They must accept the blame themselves for having rejected the salvation that God freely offered them as a free gift of His love.

1 Timothy 2:3-4 says: "This is good and pleases God our Savior, who wants all men to be saved and to come to a knowledge of the truth." If God decrees the damnation of anyone, then there is conflict between what God desires and what He decrees. In my book, *The Bible Explained,* I wrote, "In the divine nature there can be no conflict. All His actions are in perfect union."

According to Calvinism, God in His sovereignty decrees only for the sole reason that He desires to do so. If the decreed will of God is in conflict with the desired will of God, then God has decreed what is contrary to what He desires.

Does the Bible reveal any conditions for us to receive salvation? Here the Scriptures could not be more clear that faith is the condition for receiving God's gift of salvation. A gift cannot be earned but must be accepted. We must "believe in the Lord Jesus Christ" (Acts 16:31).

The Scriptures teach that election is based on foreknowledge. 1 Peter 1:2 says the elect, "Have been chosen according to the foreknowledge of God the Father." Romans 8:29 states, "For those God foreknew He also predestined to be conformed to the likeness of His Son." God foreknew who would believe and be saved.

God sent out His invitation "whosoever will" and God knew from eternity past who would accept His invitation and in turn He elected them. God's loving invitation for a relationship with Him must be freely accepted.

Please explain "total depravity." I understand it to mean that no one can believe until they are regenerated and this can only happen to God's "elect." Unbelievers are spiritually dead and the dead cannot believe, unless they are among the "elect" whom God will cause to believe. No one can believe by their own power. God must "draw" them (John 6:44).

Total depravity simply means that salvation is beyond our grasp in our own ability. But the Calvinist doctrine defines it to mean inability to even receive salvation as a free gift.

Spiritual death is separation from God. It means that we cannot work our way back to God. We cannot reach God; He must reach us. Mankind was created with a sense or instinct of God, and creation confirms this instinct. Paul declares that even though we are spiritually dead, fallen mankind can perceive the truth of God. Adam and Eve were spiritually dead after they sinned in the Garden. But they could hear the voice of God and respond to Him (Genesis 3:10).

Jesus said in John 6:44: "No one can come to me unless the Father who sent me draws him, and I will raise him up at the last day."

But in John 12:32-33 Jesus says, "But I, when I am lifted up from the earth, will draw all men unto myself. He said this to show the kind of death he was going to die."

Here Jesus says that when He is lifted up on the cross, He will draw all men to Him. The word *men* is the generic for *mankind*. This is done through the preaching of the gospel.

The Holy Spirit uses the gospel to convict men of sin and draw them to Christ. Speaking of the Holy Spirit, Jesus said in John 16:8: "When He comes, He will convict the world of guilt in regard to sin and righteousness and judgment."

So we see that everyone will be drawn by the Holy Spirit through the preaching of the gospel. This is why we read, "So, the Holy Spirit says: 'Today, if you hear his voice, do not harden your hearts'" (Hebrew 3:8,15; 4:7). We are warned not to harden our hearts when we are drawn by the Holy Spirit to see our need of Christ.

The Holy Spirit inspired the Scriptures and empowers them to bring conviction of our sins and open our dead eyes to see God's provision of a Savior to meet all our needs: "For the Word of God is living and active. Sharper than any double-edged sword, it penetrates even to dividing soul and spirit, joints and marrow; it judges the thoughts and attitudes of the heart. Nothing in all creation is hidden from God's sight. Everything is uncovered and laid bare before the eyes of Him to whom we must give account" (Hebrews 4:12).

God has provided for every need for the total depravity of the sinner and his inability to save himself. Christ's death and resurrection are the answer to all his needs. It releases the Holy Spirit to convict us of our sins and to show us our need of the Savior. All of our excuses for rejecting Christ are swept away by the Holy Spirit's conviction and enablement. And we are warned not to harden our hearts to God's provision in Christ.

Mankind's need of saving faith is provided through the Holy Spirit and the Word of God: "For everyone who calls upon the name of the Lord will be saved. How can they call on the one they have not believed in? And how can they believe in the one whom they have not heard? And how can they hear without someone preaching to them" (Romans 10:13-14).

Paul continues in verse 17: "Consequently, faith comes from hearing the message, and the message is heard through the word of Christ."

Here we see that we receive salvation through faith, and this faith comes through hearing the gospel message about Christ.

The Holy Spirit uses the message of the gospel to convict the sinner of his need of Christ, at which point the sinner can respond or resist the Holy Spirit's drawing. In Matthew 23:37, Jesus mourns over Jerusalem: "How often I have longed to gather your children together, as a hen gathers her chicks under her wings, but you were not willing." After resisting the Holy Spirit for a time, the sinner's heart becomes hardened in his rejection of Christ. At some point, this hardening of the sinner's heart will become set in his rejection of Christ. This is the unpardonable sin. At some point, the sinner becomes beyond conviction, and the Holy Spirit leaves him to himself.

To say that a person is regenerated in order to believe is to put the cart before the horse. Scripture is abundantly clear that a person must believe in order to be regenerated. Through regeneration, a person becomes a child of God. We are told in John 1:12-13: "Yet to all who received Him, to those who believed in His name, He gave the right to become the children of God – children born not of natural descent or of a husband's will, but born of God."

This is why Paul wrote in Romans 1:16, "I am not ashamed of the gospel, for it is the power of God for the salvation of everyone who believes."

The preaching of the gospel or witnessing to the gospel (good news) is the *drawing* of God. The Holy Spirit empowers the hearer to believe. Jesus referred to this in John 3:5: "I tell you the truth, no one can enter the kingdom of God unless he is born of water and the Spirit." We must go to the Word of God to see what the water here refers to. Many times *water* is associated with the Word of God and birth. The following is taken from my book, *The Bible Explained*:

> In Ephesians 5:26 we read of the "Washing of water through the Word." Then in James 1:18 we read: "He chose to give us birth through the word of truth." And in I Peter 1:23: "For you have been born again not of perishable seed but of imperishable through the living and enduring Word of God."
>
> So we see that the *water* is associated with the Word of God and with birth. Of course, Spirit refers to the Holy Spirit. The Holy Spirit uses His Word to bring about the new birth. In Romans 10:17 we read, "Consequently, faith comes from hearing the message, and the message is heard through the word of Christ."
>
> Here we see that we receive salvation by faith. But in order to have faith, you must have something to believe. When a person hears the gospel message concerning the Lord Jesus Christ, the Holy Spirit reveals Christ in such a way that the sinner can decide for Christ or harden his heart against the Holy Spirit's conviction of his or her need of Christ. Thus, those who believe are born of water (The Word of God – the Gospel message) and the Holy Spirit.

There is not one verse in the Bible that suggests that total depravity means inability to believe or that the sinner is incapable of believing the gospel and God condemns him for not believing. One must not misread Ephesians 2:1: "As for you, you were dead in your transgressions and sins." This refers to fallen mankind being separated from the life of God.

Calvinists equate spiritual death to physical death. For example, "The fallen sons of Adam are dead in sin, not just sick, not just weak, not almost dead, but dead and unable to make the slightest movement toward God."

While it is true that fallen mankind is enslaved by sin and cannot contribute any good work to earn his salvation, he can receive a free gift; he can be convicted of his sin and judgment and his need of Christ through the work of the Holy Spirit. This is the Holy Spirit's work in the world as we are told in John 16:7-9: "But I tell you the truth: It is for your good that I am going away. Unless I go away, the Counselor will not come to you; but if I go, I will send Him to you. When He comes, He will convict the world of guilt in regard to sin and righteousness and judgment: in regard to sin, because men do not believe in me."

It is strictly by the grace of God through Jesus Christ that salvation comes to the sinner, but to believe the gospel and receive a free gift from God does not contribute to the free gift; it merely accepts it. Faith is not a work nor does any credit come to the person who simply believes.

Please explain the 4th point of the acronym T.U.L.I.P. – irresistible grace. Does this mean if you are one of God's elect you will not be able to resist God's call, and if you are not one of His elect you cannot be saved?

According to Calvinism, you have stated it correctly. However, this is not the teaching of the Bible. According to Calvinism, the unregenerate elect are dead spiritually and cannot respond to the gospel message by faith. Therefore, God must regenerate them (with the new birth). And then God gives this regenerated person the faith to believe the gospel.

According to Calvinism, man can have no part in salvation, no human responsibility. While it is absolutely true that God alone can save and we cannot save ourselves by our own merits, this does not mean that man has no responsibility in salvation.

The Calvinist's viewpoint is that they have God dealing with mankind as if we were inanimate matter, by sheer force. But mankind was created with free will to obey God with their wills because forced obedience is not real obedience. God does not want a forced love for Him, a forced belief in Christ. All through the Scriptures, God pleads with mankind to make a deliberate choice to trust in Christ for salvation as a free moral being. And though mankind has suffered a devastating fall in Adam, they still know they are accountable to God in matters of right and wrong.

God's grace works with mankind's free will. It is a cooperative relationship. God invites, and man must accept. God gives, and man must accept. In God's foreknowledge, He saw who would believe and elected them and predestined them to be like the resurrected Christ.

The invitation is still going out to *whoever*: "Whoever is thirsty, let him come; and whoever wishes, let him take the free gift of the water of life" (Revelation 22:17).

While God will enable a man to do what God wants him to do, He will not make that decision for him. He can bring pressure through stern warnings or loving invitations to weigh the consequences of moral decisions, but He will not make moral decisions for us. When God created free moral beings in men and angels, he limited His control over them. Calvinists teach that God gives the gift of faith to the elect as a necessity because of mankind's depravity, which they interpret as inability to believe.

Evidence for this is taken from Ephesians 2:8-9, a sometimes- misinterpreted passage of Scripture: "For it is by grace you have been saved, through faith – and this not of yourselves, it is the gift of God – not by works, so that no one can boast." Calvinists claim that *this* refers to faith. However the Greek clears this up as *this* is neuter and cannot refer to *faith*, which is feminine in form. "It is the gift of God" refers to "saved." The "gift of God" is salvation by grace through faith. New Testament Greek scholar A. T. Robertson comments on this passage: "*grace* is God's part; *faith* ours. And it refers to the act of being saved by grace conditioned on faith on our part."

God will not force mankind's will but will encourage us to do right by the use of rewards and punishments. The Bible makes a point of this very clearly because it is essential to the understanding of evil in the world. Calvinists talk or write about, "The mystery of God's sovereignty and the existence of evil." But the Bible does not present it as a mystery.

It *would* be a great mystery if one believed that nothing can happen without God being the cause of it, including sin and evil. That would mean that God, who is holy, first ordained by divine decree that mankind would sin and then held them guilty for doing what they could not help doing (were ordained to do by divine decree). Then He would punish them with eternity in hell to show His hatred of sin.

The Bible does not present this as a mystery. It is presented very clearly that Adam and Eve rebelled against their loving Creator and brought sin and evil into the universe. And while mankind is free to war with God, he is not free to win this war. He is free to break God's laws, but he is not free to do so without punishment. Thus, there is no mystery in God's sovereignty and man's free will.

God gave mankind free will to choose to freely love Him, but they used their free will to rebel and sin against Him. But that is not all. God took humanity upon Himself to suffer and die to pay for the sins we committed against Him. But man's rebellion was to a limited area and for a limited time.

At the appointed time, our Sovereign God will bring the curtain down upon His rebellious creation and settle all accounts. And those who received by simple faith the sacrifice of the Son of God will be united to Him forever in what is called the wedding of the Lamb: "Then I heard what sounded like a great multitude, like the roar of rushing waters and like loud pearls of thunder, shouting: 'Hallelujah! for our Lord God Almighty reigns.' Let us rejoice and be glad and give Him glory! for the wedding of the Lamb has come, and the bride has made herself ready. Fine linen, bright and clean, was given to her to wear. [fine linen stands for the righteous acts of the saints]" (Revelation 19: 6-8).

But in the meantime, God sends forth His loving, gracious invitation to a vile, filthy, sinful, and depraved humanity. They need not remain under judgment because God, in His infinite love, came to this world as a man and paid for all mankind's sins; and through the work of Christ, God will change a hell-bound sinner into a heaven-bound saint. God is not mere omnipotent power, as Calvinists seem to think of Him, but a loving, personal, intimate Lord seeking His wayward creation.

By making grace irresistible and men passive agents, Calvinism seems to destroy the personal quality of the relationship between God and mankind, which is established by God's grace through Jesus Christ and involves the free response of man's will to the loving, gracious will of God.

All through Jesus' ministry, He seems to take it for granted that God's grace can be resisted.

Is God's grace irresistible? The Scriptures many times refers to God's overtures toward mankind being resisted: "0 Jerusalem, Jerusalem, you who kill the prophets and stone those sent to you, how often I have longed to gather your children together, as a hen gathers her chicks under her wings but you were not willing" (Matthew 23: 37). Jesus longed to save them, but they were not willing to respond to His willingness. The Greek is more emphatic, the Greek verb *thelo* (to will) is used both times, "I willed . . .but you were not willing." Jesus was clearly showing His frustration.

"You stiff-necked people, with uncircumcised hearts and ears! You are just like your fathers: you always resist the Holy Spirit" (Acts 7:51). Stephen told them that throughout the history of Israel, down to the time of Christ, they had resisted the Holy Spirit.

Titus 2:11 tells us, "For the grace of God that brings salvation has appeared to all men." Calvinists tell us that God's grace has appeared for a few elect, but the Word of God says it has appeared to all men.

2 Peter 3:9 tells us, "The Lord is not slow in keeping His promise, as some men understand slowness. He is patient with you, not wanting anyone to perish, but everyone to come to repentance."

The fact that believers are warned against quenching the Spirit (1 Thessalonians 5:19) and grieving the Spirit (Ephesians 4:30) clearly shows that the Holy Spirit can be resisted. This is true because the Holy Spirit is not sheer power but a loving Person whose great desire is to reveal Christ to us and empower us to live for Him.

John 5:39-40 says, "You diligently study the Scriptures because you think that by them you possess eternal life. These are the Scriptures that testify about me, yet you refuse to come to me to have life." This last phrase in the Greek is even more emphatic: "You do not will to come."

According to the Calvinist's view of God's sovereignty, God must save men before they believe. Otherwise, man will earn some of the glory for his salvation. To Calvinists, election must be unconditional, not requiring faith (which they term a good work); and grace must be irresistible, otherwise man will help in his own salvation. But as we have already seen, faith is not meritorious but simply receiving the free gift that Christ suffered and died to give us.

While it is true that the drawing work of God is necessary for salvation, the drawing, however, is not irresistible. In John 16:8 we are told what this drawing is: "When He (the Holy Spirit) comes, He will convict the world of guilt in regard to sin and righteousness and judgment." The convicting work of the Holy Spirit is done to the world.

The Bible teaches that salvation is open to all, not only to a few who are irresistibly drawn. The word for *all* in 1 Timothy 2:4 and *everyone* in 2 Peter 3:9 is the Greek word *pas*, which means exactly that – all and everyone, not a select few.

"This is good and pleases God our Savior, who wants all men to be saved and to come to the knowledge of the truth" (I Timothy 2:4).

"The Lord is not slow in keeping His promise, as some men understand slowness. He is patient with you, not wanting anyone to perish, but everyone to come to repentance" (I Peter 3:9). It is the same Greek word in 2 Timothy 3:16: "All Scripture is God-breathed" and John 1:3: "Through Him (Christ) all things were made."

The Bible specifically teaches that the Holy Spirit can be resisted and repeatedly calls on all people to respond to God's invitation.

In the parable of the sower, the emphasis is not on sowing the seed but on the reception of the seed.

Throughout Scripture, belief is the essential precondition for salvation. "For God so loved the world that He gave his one and only Son, that whoever believes in Him shall not perish but have eternal life."

If Calvinism is correct it would read the opposite: "Whosoever has eternal life will believe."

To the Philippian jailer's question, "What must I do to be saved?" Paul's answer is, "Believe in the Lord Jesus, and you will be saved." Again, belief is the condition for salvation.

Do you hold to the Calvinistic view of perseverance of the saints?

One of the major teachings of Calvinism is that persevering in good works is the assurance of salvation and the necessary evidence for salvation. The Calvinist's assurance is in the hope that God predestined them to eternal life as the elect or chosen ones. How do people know they are one of the elect who have been predestined? Only by their performance, but how do they know that their performance is living up to it?

Calling it "perseverance of the saints" puts the burden upon the believer's ability to persevere. However, salvation that begins with faith in Christ cannot end in depending on our performance. Rather than perseverance of the saints, preservation of the saints would be a better term.

A. W. Tozer said Adam lost the key to his salvation to Satan and Christ came and won the key back for Adam. When Adam held his hand out to receive the key back, Jesus closed His hand around the key and said, "I'll hold on to it this time."

"My sheep hear my voice; I know them, and they follow me. I give them eternal life, and they shall never perish; no one can snatch them out of my hand. My Father, who has given them to me, is greater than all; no one can snatch them out of my Father's hand. I and my Father are one"(John 10:27-30).

The Bible does not so much teach the perseverance of the saints as the preservation of the saints. Although the new birth and the Holy Spirit's indwelling will show itself in the believer's life, it is not based on some overpowering predestination that causes a believer to act in certain ways. It is based on the fact that believers belong to God, and He will hold on to them until He brings their salvation to completion.

"And this is the will of Him who sent me, that I should lose none of all that He has given me, but raise them up at the last day. For my Father's will is that everyone who looks to the Son and believes in him shall have eternal life, and I will raise him up at the last day" (John 6:39-40).

"All that the Father gives me will come to me, and whoever comes to me I will never drive away" (John 6:37).

"And do not grieve the Holy Spirit of God, with whom you were sealed for the day of redemption" (Ephesians 4:30).

"And I will ask the Father, and He will give you another counselor to be with you forever" (John 14:16).

"I tell you the truth, whoever hears my word and believes Him who sent me has eternal life and will not be condemned; he has crossed over from death to life" (John 5:24).

Assurance is part of saving faith based upon the Word of God. Saving faith, of course, will persevere because of regeneration and the Holy Spirit living in us. Perseverance is a promise because of the Holy Spirit's indwelling, not a requirement.

The believer does not serve God out of legalism but out of love and thankfulness.

Perseverance of the faith is clearly presented in 1 John 5:4: "For everyone born of God overcomes the world. This is the victory that has overcome the world, even our faith. Who is it that overcomes the world? Only he who believes that Jesus is the Son of God."

God's keeping of the believer is presented in Roman 8:31-39: "What then shall we say in regard to this? If God be for us, who can be against us? He who did not spare His own Son, but gave Him up for us all – how will He not also, along with Him, graciously give us all things? Who will bring any charge against those whom God has chosen? It is God who justifies; who is he that condemns? Christ Jesus, who died – more than that, who was raised to life – is at the right hand of God and is also interceding for us. Who shall separate us from the love of Christ? Shall trouble or hardship or persecution or famine or nakedness or danger or sword? As it is written: 'For your sake we face death all day long; we are considered as sheep to be slaughtered.'

"No, in all these things we are more than conquerors through Him who loved us. For I am convinced that neither life nor death, neither angels nor demons, neither the present nor the future, nor any powers, neither height nor depth, nor anything else in all creation, will be able to separate us from the love of God that is in Christ Jesus our Lord."

The indwelling Holy Spirit is the guarantee that no backslider has peace. God promises to finish what He has begun. "Being confident of this, that He who began a good work in you will carry it on to completion until the day of Christ Jesus" (Philippians 1:6).

Perseverance is a faith that cannot be destroyed but persists until it is replaced by sight. Saving faith will manifest itself during our journey of discipleship. It may stumble and fall but it will not stay down; it will get back up and never leave the trail until we see the One who called us. Perseverance is not so much a requirement as a promise that the One who called you will not fail to bring you home into His presence.

"And you also were included in Christ when you heard the word of truth, the gospel of your salvation. Having believed you were marked with a seal, the promised Holy Spirit, who is a deposit guaranteeing our inheritance until the redemption of those who are God's possession – to the praise of His glory" (Ephesians 1:13).

This tells us that as soon as we believe, we are marked by the presence of the Holy Spirit as God's property.

Please explain limited atonement. Does the Bible teach this? If so, who is it limited to?

Limited atonement along with total depravity (as inability), unconditional election, and irresistible grace are misinterpretations of Scripture. Limited atonement denies the clear Scriptural teaching that God loves everyone who makes up the *world*.

The teaching of *total depravity* as inability to believe in and trust Christ makes necessary the teaching of *unconditional election* – that God has chosen or elected certain ones, from eternity past, to be sovereignly regenerated unconditionally, for no reason (such as faith). *Limited atonement* means that Christ died only for those elected from eternity past.

If Christ died for all men, including those who will not believe, whom God did not choose from eternity past, His blood would have been "spilt in vain." If the Calvinist doctrine that Christ's redeeming work was intended to save only certain persons but not every person, then His death was a failure. Calvinists believe that if Jesus died for every person, then the real saving power is not in the blood, but rather the power would be in the will of the creature.

That is like saying if someone gave me money to pay off a debt and I accepted the money and paid the debt off, that the credit for paying off the debt would go to me for accepting the money rather than to the one who gave me the money.

My faith has no power and cannot contribute to salvation that Christ purchased for me and God offers freely in the Gospel, but it simply receives what Christ purchased and God offers to me as a free gift. Calvinists infer that if you so much as hold out your hand to receive salvation, you have earned it. But how does one earn a free gift?

Calvinists say that God is sovereign and does whatsoever He wants to do, including choosing those He wants to save. Not everyone thus can be saved, but only those He chooses. As to Scripture saying that God wants all men to be saved, they indicate that God mysteriously does not save those He doesn't want to be saved. Their explanation to this dilemma is, "It is hidden in the mystery of God's will." But God's will is revealed to us in that He wants all mankind to be saved. This, of course, contradicts limited atonement.

It is difficult to reconcile Calvinism with the Word of God without enhancing Scripture. To say that God decreed in eternity past that certain ones would reject the gospel; and then, when in actual time these do reject the gospel, He punishes them eternally. This does not reflect a God of infinite mercy who wishes all to come to Him. No, Christ died for all men, even for those who eventually choose not to be saved.

Isaiah 53:6 says, "We all, like sheep, have gone astray, each of us has turned to his own way; and the Lord has laid on him the iniquity of us all."

Who went astray? Was it all mankind or only the elect? If only the elect went astray, then it was only for them that Christ had to die. But if it was all of mankind who went astray, then it was the iniquity of all mankind that was laid on Him.

Romans 5:6 tells us, "At just the right time, when we were still powerless, Christ died for the ungodly." Christ died for the ungodly. Was all mankind ungodly or only the elect?

When you follow Calvinist thought, if Christ's death was intended to save all men, then it must have failed. Calvinists don't accept the fact that Christ's death was intended only for those who would receive Him. Romans 6:23 tells us, "For the wages of sin is death, but the gift of God is eternal life in Jesus Christ our Lord." Notice that what we have earned is death. Eternal life is a gift from God. God gives the gift freely but it must be appreciated and accepted. Gifts cannot be forced on people but must be accepted.

John 1:10-12 says, "He was in the world, and though the world was made through Him, the world did not recognize Him. He came to that which was His own, but His own did not receive Him. Yet to all who received Him, to those who believed in His name, He gave the right to become the children of God."

Christ died for all men but this must be received by faith. In 1 Timothy 4:10, Paul tells us why he labored so hard to spread the gospel:

"This is a trustworthy saying that deserves full acceptance (and for this we labor and strive), that we have put our hope in the living God, who is the Savior of all men, and especially of those who believe."

Christ died for all men and is potentially the Savior of the whole world in general, but He is the actual Savior of those who believe.

But Calvinists say faith is a good work and we cannot be saved by good works. This is contradicted by Ephesians 2:8-9, where faith and works are contrasted: "For it is by grace you have been saved, through faith – and this not of yourselves, it is the gift of God – not by works, so that no one can boast."

Salvation is a gift from God and must be accepted through faith. Faith has no merit but is simply the hand that accepts the gift of eternal life. John 3:16-18 clearly states that salvation and condemnation are conditioned on the sinner's reaction to God's provision of salvation through Christ: "For God so loved the world that He gave His one and only Son, that whoever believes in Him shall not perish but have eternal life. For God did not send His Son into the world to condemn the world, but to save the world through Him. Whoever believes in Him is not condemned, but whoever does not believe stands condemned already because he has not believed in the name of God's one and only Son." Christ's atonement is limited to those who believe in Him.

In an attempt to support limited atonement, Calvinists use Scriptures that they say prove that Christ only died for a limited number. Matthew 20:28 is used to say that Christ did not die for all but only for many: "Just as the Son of Man did not come to be served, but to serve, and to give his life a ransom for many." Ephesians 5:25 is used to show that He did not die for all but only for the church: "Husbands, love your wives, just as Christ loved the church and gave Himself up for her."

Of course, if Christ died for all, as a multitude of verses tell us, then of course He died for "many," and for the "church." Paul, in Galatians 2:20 says that Christ died for him: "The life I live in the body, I live by faith in the Son of God, who loved me and gave Himself for me." Does this prove that Christ did not die for all but only for Paul?

Must we say, according to Romans 5:15, not all but only many fell when Adam fell? "But the gift is not like the trespass. For if the many died by the trespass of one man, how much more did God's grace and the gift that came by the grace of the one man, Jesus Christ, overflow to the many."

Are the Scriptures the perfect and infallible Word of God, or can they be enhanced to accommodate someone's theology? Here are some statements by noted Calvinists. Edwin Palmer says, referring to John 3:16, "It is just because God so loved the world of elect sinners that He sent His only begotten Son that the world might be saved through Him" (John 3:16-17). In this case, Palmer adds the word "elect" to enhance Scripture, limiting God's love to a few (Edwin H. Palmer, *The Five Points of Calvinism*).

Loraine Boettner says, "Again it was not the whole of mankind which was equally loved by God." (*The Reformed Doctrine of Predestination*).

A.W. Pink in *The Sovereignty of God* writes: "That God loves everybody, is, we may say, quite a modern belief ... To tell the Christ-rejecting that God loves him is to cauterize his conscience ... There is far too much presenting of Christ to sinners today." This is what happens when Calvinism is taken to its extremes.

Let's listen to what Jesus Himself says: "What do you think? If a man owns a hundred sheep, and one of them wanders away, will he not leave the ninety and nine on the hills and go to look for the one that wandered off? And if he finds it, I tell you the truth, he is happier about that one sheep than about the ninety and nine that did not wander off. In the same way your Father in heaven is not willing that any of these little ones should be lost"(Matthew 18:12-14).

To answer your last question, "who was the atonement limited to?" it is limited to sinners – the whole human race. The atoning work of

Christ was unlimited in its extent (all mankind) but limited in its application (those who believe in Christ).

John 3:16 tells us: "For God so loved the world that He gave His one and only Son, that whoever believes in him shall not perish but have eternal life" (John 3:16). Calvinists say "world" here refers to the elect. But verse 19 refutes this: "This is the verdict: Light has come into the world, but men loved darkness instead of light because their deeds were evil." This is clearly the fallen world.

If world means only the elect, then Romans 3:23, "All have sinned and come short of the glory of God" would refer to the elect only, but that is not what the Scripture says.

What do election and predestination mean? Do they mean that men do not have free will?

Election refers to God's choice of who will be saved. Predestination has to do with the end result of God's election. Romans 8:28-30 clearly states that both election and predestination are based upon God's foreknowledge. It is all summed up in verse 29: "For those God foreknew He also predestined to be conformed to the likeness of His Son, that he might be the firstborn among many brothers." This makes the whole process of salvation clear and easy to understand, including man's free will which is also clearly taught in Scripture. Children can actually grasp it if they take the Scriptures at face value. The problem comes when men try to force the Scriptures to conform to their theological system, rather than their theologies conforming to Scripture.

God, who knows all things, knows who will believe the gospel and trust Christ. God chooses these people for salvation based on His foreknowledge. God then unites them forever with Christ and predestinates them to be glorified in the likeness of the Lord Jesus Christ.

There is no conflict between God's sovereignty and man's free will. Simply put, in His sovereignty God has chosen to work with man's free will. God does not want a heaven filled with robots who love Him simply because they were programmed to love Him. Mankind's free will was necessary for God's purpose for mankind. Love must be chosen freely and this requires free will.

Doesn't teaching that a person is saved simply by believing make salvation a form of easy-believism and cheapens the whole concept of salvation?

Easy-believism is belief with no commitment. If by believing you mean simply believing certain facts about Jesus, then you are not speaking of Biblical believing. Paul and James clearly bring this out in what some say is a contradiction between them, but there isn't. Paul states the clear teaching of the Scriptures that a person is saved by faith without works. James does not contradict this truth but simply defines what saving faith is. Saving faith brings a change of life to a person. Salvation is by faith alone, but it is not a dead faith but a living faith that is active and motivates those saved to do good works. James asks, "What good is it, my brothers, if a man claims to have faith but has no deed? Can such faith save him?" (James 2:14). Anyone can claim to have faith, but a change of life is the proof.

"Show me your faith without deeds, and I will show you my faith by what I do. You believe that there is one God. Good! Even the demons believe that – and shudder" (James 2: 18-19).

Here James is showing two kinds of faith. One is a simple head knowledge with no commitment. Even the demons have this faith. They know there is one God and they shudder because they know they will be judged by Him.

Saving faith comes from the conviction of sin and moves a person to turn from his sins and commit himself to Christ as his refuge from God's righteous judgment. It is a commitment to Christ as Lord and Savior. You have made a complete about-face. Once you were number one in your life, but now Christ is; this is true repentance.

You still have much to learn about serving Him, but a fundamental change has taken place in your life. In one sense, you are still the same person, but in another sense everything has changed. The essence of faith is reliance upon God and a commitment of yourself to Him forever. Faith has no merit; it is simply the hand that accepts the free gift of eternal life from the One who suffered and died to give it to you.

Please explain repentance and faith. I have heard ministers sometimes say to be saved you have to have faith. At other times I heard them say you have to repent to be saved. What's the difference between repentance and faith?
Repentance is more than simply feeling sorry or regret; it is a change of mind and purpose of life. Repentance and faith are two sides of the same coin. It means a complete about-face, a total change of direction of life. It is the turning from a life centered around self and turning to a life centered in Christ. It is a radical, fundamental change of heart that leads to a whole new direction of life. You are still the same person in one way, but you are a totally different person in another way. It is

a permanent change brought about by regeneration (new birth from above, a new relationship with God forged by Jesus Christ and signed in His blood).

This is explained in 1 John 3:1: "How great is the love the Father has lavished upon us, that we should be called the children of God! And that is what we are! The reason the world does not know us is that they do not know Him."

Please explain atonement and the Mosaic sacrificial system.
The Mosaic sacrificial system was a type or a representation of the coming Messiah who would pay the ultimate sacrifice for sin. In the temple, God's throne rested upon the tablets of the Law, which had been broken by mankind. Thus, the throne of God was a throne of judgment.

When the sacrificial blood was applied to the broken law, symbolizing that judgment had been carried out, God's throne of judgment became a throne of mercy.

This is why we are told in Colossians 2:17 concerning the Old Testament rituals: "These are a shadow of the things that were to come; the reality, however, is found in Christ."

These sacrifices and rituals pictured the coming Messiah, who threw His shadow on the wall of history as He approached. We read, at the death of Christ on the cross that, "The curtain of the temple was torn from top to bottom, the earth shook and the rocks split" (Matthew 27:51).

It is emphasized that the curtain was torn from top to bottom, rather than from the bottom up, showing that it was not torn by the earthquake, but by the hand of God. This curtain separated the holy of holies through which the high priest would enter once a year with blood on the Day of Atonement.

The holy of holies was where God's symbolic presence, the Shekinah Glory, dwelt. This opening to the holy of holies at the death of Christ indicated that from now on, it was through Christ that man has access to God.

This is explained in Hebrews 10:11-12: "Day after day every priest stands and performs his religious duties; again and again he offers the same sacrifices, which can never take away sins. But when this priest had offered for all time one sacrifice for sin, he sat down at the right hand of God."

Here we see that the Old Testament priests stood daily offering sacrifices over and over again that could not take away sin but only typified and pointed to the One who would (verse 11). But this man, Jesus Christ, offered one sacrifice (only one perfect sacrifice that fulfilled all the Old Testament sacrifices – the sacrifice of Himself) and sat down at the right hand of God.

After only one sacrifice, this Priest "sat down" because, as He said from the cross, "It is finished," or "paid in full." Hebrews 10:14 adds: "Because by one sacrifice He has made perfect forever those who are being made holy." By His one sacrifice, Christ made atonement (mercy seated God). God's throne of judgment has been made a throne of mercy.

Is healing in the atonement?

Yes, healing is in the atonement. Christ died to bring us physical as well as spiritual healing but not the way most people think. Romans 8:22-23 reads: "We know that the whole creation has been groaning as in the pains of childbirth right up to the present time. Not only so, but we ourselves, who have the first fruits of the Spirit, groan inwardly as we wait eagerly for our adoption as sons, the redemption of our bodies."

So we see that the first fruits of the Spirit is the new birth of our inner man, our spirit. This is the first fruits of what Christ purchased for us while we eagerly wait for the completion of our salvation, the redemption of our bodies, which Christ purchased for us in the atonement. This will be permanent healing.

Can Christians lose their salvation? Is once saved always saved a true doctrine of the Bible?

First of all, what do you mean by *Christian*? There are many imitations. 2 Timothy 3:5 speaks of, "Having a form of godliness but denying its power." This refers to people who have the appearance of being a Christian but not the power or reality of the Holy Spirit living in them. We are told in Romans 8:9, "If anyone does not have the Spirit of Christ, he does not belong to Christ." Many claim to be saved who really are not. Only those who are truly born again have the Holy Spirit living in them and Jesus said in John 14:16 that the Holy Spirit will indwell believers "forever."

Judas Iscariot was one of those who had the *form* or *appearance* of being a Christian and was not. Some claim that Judas was saved and lost his salvation but this is in error. We see this in John 6:70-71: "Then Jesus replied, 'Have I not chosen you, the twelve? Yet one of you is a devil!' (He meant Judas, the son of Simon Iscariot, who, though one of the twelve, was later to betray Him.)"

Then in John 13:10-11 Jesus speaking to His disciples says, "'And you are clean, though not every one of you.' For He knew who was going to betray Him, and that was why He said not every one was clean." So we see that while Judas had the appearance of a believer, he was not. There was no reality in his relationship to Christ. So Judas, rather than losing his salvation, simply never had it to begin with.

In Matthew 7:23, Jesus says to those who thought they were saved but were not, "Then I will tell them plainly, 'I never knew you.'" He will not say, "I once knew you, but now I don't."

In John 15:5-6, Jesus is referring to fruit-bearing, not salvation. He is using the analogy of a branch not remaining connected to the vine and being unable to bear fruit. This refers to a believer not in fellowship with Christ. Branches that are disconnected from the vine are useless as far as fruit-bearing. They are pruned off and used for fuel for the ovens. The point is that Christians who do not remain in fellowship with Christ are useless because "Apart from me you can do nothing."

Believers out of fellowship grieve the Holy Spirit and block His flow of power, just as branches disconnected from the vine lose the life-giving flow of sap from the vine and cannot bear fruit.

In 1 John 2:19 we read, "They went out from us, but they did not really belong to us. For if they had belonged to us, they would have remained with us; but their going showed that none of them belonged to us." Here we read of unbelievers who appeared to be Christians but were not and eventually fell away because they were not true believers.

The person who truly puts his faith in Christ has entered into a relationship that will span the ages of eternity. Salvation is not something we have to earn or struggle to hang on to. It is a gift from God based upon what Christ did on our behalf. Christ has already done everything to provide our salvation, and that's why we simply have to believe in

Him and receive the gift of eternal life: "For the wages of sin is death, but the gift of God is eternal life in Christ Jesus our Lord."

Note that what we have all earned for our sins is death. This is eternal death away from the presence of God, in suffering and loneliness. But Christ took our wages that we have earned, and He suffered and died for us. And God has replaced the wages that we have earned with a gift purchased by Jesus Christ. It cannot be earned. A gift must simply be accepted. Simply trusting Jesus is the hand that receives the gift of eternal life.

In John 10:27-30, Jesus says to those who trust Him, "My sheep listen to my voice; I know them and they follow me. I give them eternal life, and they shall never perish; no one can snatch them out of my hand. My Father, who has given them to me, is greater than all; no one can snatch them out of my Father's hand. I and my Father are one." The believer is too precious to Him to allow anyone to take them away from Him.

Jesus loves us too much and has paid too dear a price to allow us to lose our salvation. We are given the assurance by God Himself: "He that has begun a good work in you [this refers to the work of salvation when we trusted in Christ] will carry it on to completion until the day of Jesus Christ" (Philippians 1:6).

God has chosen all those who would believe in Christ and predestined them to be adopted as His children, to spend eternity with Him in a love relationship that will never end: "Praise be to the God and Father of our Lord Jesus Christ, who has blessed us in the heavenly realms with every spiritual blessing in Christ. For He chose us in Him before the creation of the world to be holy and blameless in His sight. In love, He predestined us to be adopted as His sons through

Jesus Christ in accordance with His pleasure and will – to the praise of His glorious grace, which He has freely given us in the One he loves" (Ephesians 1:3-6).

But the doctrine of eternal security does not mean that a believer can live any way he wants and not be held accountable. God disciplines His children in this life and they will have to stand before the judgment seat of Christ to give an account of what they did with their lives after being saved (Romans 3:10-12; 1 Corinthians 3:9-15).

What does the Bible mean when it says Christians are sealed by the Holy Spirit?

The answer to this question is found in Ephesians 4:30: "And do not grieve the Holy Spirit of God, with whom you are sealed for the day of redemption."

This sealing with the Holy Spirit takes place the moment a person trusts in Christ. The seal is a Person, the Holy Spirit, who will live in us forever: "And I will ask the Father, and He will give you another Counselor to be with you forever – the Spirit of truth" (John 14:16-17).

The Holy Spirit is God's seal of ownership, the sign of a completed transaction. It is the pledge (or down payment) that God will fulfill all His promises to the believer. Christ paid the entire purchase price so the Holy Spirit can move within the body of the believer, and this guarantees that He will fulfill the rest of the promises He has made.

God indwells believers (in the Person of the Holy Spirit) and lives within them while He fulfills the rest of His pledge. While believers in Christ have received many of the blessings now (they are born again, have been given eternal life, and have become children of God), they are waiting to receive the completion of their salvation (the glorification of their bodies and the removal of all the effects of sin). Believers are removed from the penalty of sin and are waiting to be removed from the presence of sin. In the meantime, we all have work to do. We are called to represent Christ until he calls us home and fulfills the rest of His promises.

The down payment and the sealing of the Holy Spirit are vitally connected and are both presented in the following verses: "Now it is God who makes both us and you stand firm in Christ. He anointed us, set His seal of ownership on us, and put His Spirit in our hearts as a deposit (or down payment) guaranteeing what is to come (2 Corinthians 1:21-22).

"And you also were included in Christ when you heard the word of truth, the gospel of salvation. Having believed, you were marked in Him with a seal, the promised Holy Spirit, who is a deposit guaranteeing our inheritance until the redemption of those who are God's possession – to the praise of His glory" (Ephesians 1:13-14).

3. End Times

What happens to us when we die?

Here we have the two eternal destinies of mankind: that of the saved and the unsaved. The souls of believers who die go immediately to be with the Lord. "For to me, to live is Christ, and to die is gain" (Philippians 1:21).

Many think of death as the end of life. But the Biblical definition of death is *separation*. The soul is separated from the body. A good analogy is a radio that runs on batteries. The batteries give the radio life. Apart from its source of life the radio is dead. The soul is the source of life for the body. It is what animates and controls the body.

When you remove the batteries from the radio, the radio dies. The life or batteries did not die but were simply removed from the radio, and the radio ceased functioning. At death, the soul (the life of the body) is simply removed from the body and goes to another place, and the body ceases to function. The body dies; the soul, the person inside the body, does not die. It simply goes to another place: for the believer that place is heaven, which is "gain" (Philippians 1:21).

Unlike the death of the unsaved, concerning which God says, "surely as I live, declares the Sovereign Lord, I take no pleasure in the death of the wicked" (Ezekiel 33: 11). God says concerning believers,

"Precious in the sight of the Lord is the death of His saints." God has no pleasure in the torment of the unsaved, but the death of His saints is precious in His sight.

The word *precious* means *valuable*. When the believer departs to be with the Lord, he or she is valuable to God. They enhance His joy and bring Him glory, while the death of the unsaved is a sad waste of a soul created in His image.

Heaven is a city built and prepared by God for His people. By faith, Abraham gave up the things of this world because he had his heart set on that heavenly city: "For he was looking toward the city with foundations, whose architect and builder is God" (Hebrews 11:10).

Concerning His people who are pilgrims on the earth with no real home here, we are told, "instead, they were longing for a better country – a heavenly one. Therefore God is not ashamed to be called their God, for He has prepared a city for them" (Hebrews 11:16).

But the Father is not content merely to have His people in the same city with Him. He has a place prepared for them in His own house. "In My Father's house are many rooms … I am going there to prepare a place for you" (John 14: 2). Believers, as God's children, have rooms in their Father's house.

Heaven is where God's people have their inheritance through Jesus Christ: "Into an inheritance that can never perish, spoil or fade – kept in heaven for you" (I Peter 1:4). Our inheritance can never perish, spoil, or fade away. It is kept in heaven for us.

Before entering into our final eternal state, our spirits in heaven will be reunited with our resurrected and glorified bodies. Then believers will stand before the judgment seat of Christ to receive rewards, apart from salvation, for what they did for Christ after being saved. Salvation is by faith alone.

In heaven will be the absence of everything bad. "He will wipe every tear from their eyes. There will be no more death or mourning or crying or pain, for the old order of things has passed away" (Revelation 21:4).

Heaven is not a place where we will float around on clouds playing harps but a place of activity and service: "No longer will there be any curse. The throne of God and of the Lamb will be in the city, and His servants shall serve Him" (Revelation 22:30).

It will be a place of rest. "Then I heard a voice from heaven say, 'Write this: Blessed are the dead who die in the Lord from now on. Yes,' says the Spirit, 'they shall rest from their labor, for their deeds will follow them'" (Revelation 14:13). Resting from our labors does not mean we will be inactive. The word "labor" here means a stressful and painful exertion. It is not work and service that will cease, but its stressfulness and painfulness. Work and service in heaven will be joyous and fulfilling.

Best of all, we will be with God: "They shall see His face and their name will be on their foreheads" (Revelation 22:4). Believers should delight in the thought of heaven, where they will be truly satisfied forever.

Their citizenship is already there: "But our citizenship is in heaven. And we eagerly await a Savior from there, the Lord Jesus Christ" (Philippians 3:20).

The place where the unsaved go at death is called *Sheol* in the Hebrew language and *Hades* in the Greek language. This is the intermediate state between death and the judgment of the Great White Throne, where they will receive their final sentence. It can be compared to our local jail where inmates wait for trial and final sentencing after all the evidence is brought in. This will include not only their works while alive but also the influence of their lives after they died.

This is where the souls of the unsaved go immediately after death. They will not receive their final sentencing until a thousand years after believers go before the Judgment Seat of Christ, when the influence of their lives will be taken into account.

For instance, a man may influence others to do evil or to disregard God, and they in turn will influence others on down through the generations until the final judgment. This intermediate state of the unsaved dead is not as terrible as the Lake of Fire, which is their final destination. But it is still a place of unimaginable suffering. In Luke 16:19-31 Jesus gives us a glimpse into this horrible place.

In verses 23-27, it is described as a place of "torment," a place of "agony," and a place where they plead for a drop of water. In verses 27-31, it is a place where they do not want their loved ones to go.

And on top of all this, they are waiting to go to another place that is far worse, where they will spend eternity!

A thousand years later, their souls will be united with their bodies that will be resurrected and tailor-made to suffer forever and never die and they will go before "the Great White Throne Judgment" of Revelation (20:11-15): "Then I saw a great white throne and Him who was seated on it. Earth and sky fled from His presence, and there was no place for them. And I saw the dead, great and small, standing before the throne, and books were opened. Another book was opened, which is the book of life. The dead were judged according to what they had done as recorded in the books. The sea gave up the dead that were in it, and death and hades gave up the dead that were in it, and each person was judged according to what he had done. Then death and Hades were thrown into the lake of fire. The lake of fire is the second death. If anyone's name was not found written in the book of life, he was thrown into the lake of fire."

Here is the final judgment of the unsaved dead. It is called the Great White Throne because it represents the absolute holiness of God. In verse 12, the "books" are opened. These are the records of each life. It's not stated in Scripture, but I believe these books will include a book of thoughts, a book of words, a book of deeds, a book of motives, and a book of influence on others, etc.

The "book of life" will be opened to show that their names are not there because they have never received Jesus as Savior and Lord. This is the book that will determine their eternal destination (verse 15).

Then these other "books" will determine the degree of their punishment. In verse 13, death and Hades gave up the dead. Here death refers to the grave, the place of their bodies, and Hades refers to where their souls were. Body and soul will be united. Then body and soul will be thrown into the lake of fire.

Here the word for lake of fire is "Gehennah," a place of eternal fire, darkness, sorrows, and where there is no rest forever.

Please explain Revelation 20:11-15. Is this literal or figurative?

This is a literal description of the unbeliever's judgment.

This passage of Scripture reads: "Then I saw a great white throne and him who was seated on it. Earth and sky fled from his presence, and there was no place for them. And I saw the dead, great and small, standing before the throne, and books were opened. Another book was opened, which is the book of life. The dead were judged according to what they had done as recorded in the books. The sea gave up the dead that were in it, and death and Hades gave up the dead that were in them, and each person was judged according to what he had done. Then death and hades were thrown into the lake of fire. The lake of fire is the second death. If anyone's name was not found written in the book of life, he was thrown into the lake of fire."

This is the final judgment of the unsaved dead. It is the most terrifying scene imaginable. It is the place where all those who have rejected the Lord Jesus Christ will stand, covered with their sins, before a holy God.

In verse 11, it is called the "great white throne," because it represents the absolute holiness of God. Heaven and earth must flee away at His presence. And all the unsaved will stand in open space before the God of the universe.

In verse 12, the "books" (plural) are opened. These contain the records of each person's life.

The "book (singular) of life" will be opened to show that their names are not there, because they have never received Jesus Christ as Savior and Lord. This is the Book that determines their eternal destiny (verse 15). Then, these other books will determine the degree of punishment.

In verse 13, "death and Hades gave up the dead that were in them." "Death" refers to the grave, the place of their bodies. "Hades" refers to the place of lost souls. Their bodies and souls will be reunited.

In verse 14, the whole person, body and soul, will be cast into the lake of fire. And this will be the eternal destiny of all those who reject Jesus Christ.

Do pets go to heaven? Do animals have souls?

Mankind and animals both were created from the earth and for the earth. That they were created from the earth is seen in Genesis 2:7,19: "The Lord formed the man from the dust of the ground and breathed into his nostrils the breath of life, and the man became a living soul." And Genesis 2:19: "Now the Lord God had formed out of the ground all the beasts of the field and all the birds of the air."

Both have souls – "the breath of life" and soul are described by the same Hebrew word *Nephesh*. Humans' souls are cited in Genesis 2:7: "The Lord God formed the man from the dust of the ground and breathed into his nostrils the breath of life, and the man became a living being." Animals' souls are mentioned in Genesis 1:30: "And to all the beasts of the earth and all the birds of the air and all the creatures that move on the ground – everything that has the breath of life in it – I give every green plant for food."

And they were created for the earth: "It was not to angels that he has subjected the world to come, about which we are speaking. But there is a place where someone has testified, 'What is man that you are mindful of him, and the son of man that you care for him? You made him a little lower than the angels; you crowned him with glory and honor and put everything under his feet'" (Hebrews 2:5-8).

"In putting everything under them, God left nothing that is not subject to them. Yet at present we do not see everything subject to them. But we see Jesus, who was made a little lower than the angels, now crowned with glory and honor because He suffered death, so that by the grace of God He might taste death for everyone" (Hebrews 2:8-9).

Here we are told that mankind was created to share in God's rule over the earth. The first step in this was to put the animal creation under Adam's authority. In Genesis 2:20, God caused the animals to pass before Adam so he could name them as a sign of his authority over them.

But mankind sinned and lost their authority over the world to Satan who became the "prince of this world" (John 12:31). But Jesus took upon Himself humanity and succeeded where Adam failed (John 12:31).

In Colossians 1:19-20, we read concerning Christ: "For God was pleased to have His fullness dwell in Him, and through Him to reconcile to Himself all things, whether things on earth or things in heaven, by making peace through His blood, shed on the cross."

Here we see that the "reconciling to himself all things" goes as far as the fall and curse. It covers mankind, nature, and the earth. All will be restored to God's original "very good" before sin entered in. For all creation longs for and anticipates the resurrection of God's children as we are told in Romans 8:19-23: "The creation waits in eager expectations, for the sons of God to be revealed. For the creation was subjected to frustration, not by its own choice, but by the will of the one who subjected it, in hope that the creation itself will be liberated from its bondage to decay, and brought into the glorious freedom of the children of God. We know that the whole creation has been groaning in the pains of childbirth right up to the present time. Not only so, but we ourselves, who have the first fruits of the Spirit, groan inwardly as we wait eagerly for our adoption as sons, the redemption of our bodies."

The believer's resurrection depends on Christ's resurrection: "Because I live, you also will live" (John 14:19). And we see in Romans 8:19-21 that the rest of creation depends on the resurrection of mankind: "The creation waits in eager expectations for the sons of God to be revealed. For the creation was subjected to frustration, not by its own choice, but by the will of the one who subjected it, in hope that the creation itself will be liberated from its bondage to decay and brought into the glorious freedom of the children of God."

Here we see that the redemption of believers' bodies will not only bring deliverance to them but also to the rest of creation over which mankind is the head. The earth will be renewed as our eternal home. These have been groaning in suffering though having never committed sin. These will join God's children in deliverance from the bondage of death and decay.

At the beginning of creation, before sin entered, God filled the earth with animals under mankind. When Noah left the ark after the worldwide flood to rule the new earth, God filled it again with animals. When Jesus, the Last Adam, came into the world, He was laid in a manger, a feeding trough for animals in a stable surrounded by animals. And they would have brought the infant many smiles and giggles. And when God renews the earth, he will fill it with animals no longer under the curse, to dwell with glorified mankind.

As a result of Christ's victory, mankind will be restored to his original position before sin entered the earth. Mankind's creation was unique. It was both spiritual, connecting us to God, and physical, connecting us to the animals and the earth. Mankind was created from the earth and for the earth and in the image of God to rule the glorified earth for God's glory.

Mankind and animals are forever linked in God's purpose. This is why the animal creation fell under the curse with mankind when we fell, even though they had never sinned. And this is why the curse will be lifted from the creation when mankind is liberated from the curse of the fall (Romans 8:18-20).

God has a glorious future for both mankind and the earth when the curse is lifted and the heavenly city descends to the earth (Revelation 21:1-5).

The paradise that was lost through the first Adam will be regained by the Last Adam, Jesus Christ. "For as in Adam all die, so in Christ all will be made alive" (I Corinthians 15:22).

What evidence is there that Jesus rose from the dead? It just doesn't happen. Dead men simply do not rise from the dead. That is exactly the point! Dead men do not rise from the dead – until Jesus Christ. This was the moving of God to lift the curse from mankind of sin and death. We were helpless and doomed, but God entered into our hopeless situation to provide us a way back to Him.

In 1 Corinthians 15:3-8 Paul names several eye-witnesses of the resurrected Christ, many of whom were still alive and could be questioned at that time.

The fact that the tomb was empty that first Easter morning is indisputable. That left only two options. The tomb was empty because the body was stolen or because Jesus rose from the dead. Who would have taken it? There are only two options: either His enemies or His friends.

Why would His enemies take it? Maybe as a prank or some other perverse reason? If so, then they would have been in the enviable position to refute the claim that He rose from the dead and make a laughing stock of His disciples. Why didn't they? Because they couldn't. It's that simple.

What about His disciples? For one thing, there was a Roman guard posted outside the tomb (Matthew 27:65). The guard consisted of four well-trained soldiers who would be relieved every six hours.

Imagine stepping over these soldiers and rolling away the huge stone, weighing up to two tons, without waking them, even if they were fast asleep. These soldiers would have forfeited their lives to a cruel death for allowing the Roman seal to be broken, for which they were responsible. The watch was too short of a time to worry about trained soldiers falling asleep, especially all of them! And if anyone were caught breaking the Roman seal and trying to steal the body, it would mean a torturous death.

Rome was an occupying army, and they ruled with an iron fist. The disciples did not want to be anywhere near a Roman soldier. They were not interested in taking Jesus' body. They were interested in their own safety. If Rome had executed their leader, how far away could their arrests be?

If His disciple had stolen His body, would they have gone all over the Mediterranean world preaching His resurrection, facing torture and death? Would they have been willing to die for what they would have known was a lie? People may die for what they think is true but not for what they know is a lie!

Shortly after Jesus had been executed as a criminal and His disciples were on the run, something happened that changed the Christian movement from facing extinction to a movement exploding like wildfire. Something transformed His disciples from hiding behind closed doors to fearlessly facing death by boldly facing their enemies with the claim that Jesus rose from the dead.

At the time of Jesus' crucifixion, His disciples were filled with hopeless despair and fear. Peter, the leader of the disciples, denied that he knew Jesus with oaths and curses; but a few days later, this same man and all the others faced the wrath of Rome with unshakeable courage.

Nothing natural can account for the change in Paul who was transformed from a hater and persecutor of Christians to an apostle of Jesus Christ. Paul first came upon the scene as a persecutor of Christ who was suddenly converted by the resurrected Savior Himself. He disappeared to Arabia to prepare for his ministry, where he was taught by the risen Lord. Then he reappeared to proclaim the message of a risen Savior with the same intensity that he once fought against it.

Paul traded his high position of wealth and respect as a Pharisee for poverty, persecution, and prison. Paul had met the resurrected Savior and served Him for 25 years and was used by God to write a third of the New Testament. He and the other apostles who were commissioned by the resurrected Christ to preach the gospel faced persecution and torture until they were executed, sealing their testimony with their blood. This is further evidence for the resurrection of Jesus Christ.

Is reincarnation a reality? Does the Bible teach it?

Reincarnation is a prominent teaching in Hinduism, also called the *transmigration of souls*, where the person who dies is reborn into another life either on this earth or somewhere in the many heavens and hells of Hinduism. Furthermore, it may be as a human being, animal, insect, or even a vegetable. This is determined by the law of karma (meaning *deeds*); the tallying up of a person's deeds in his lifetime will determine a person's rebirth after death.

This process goes on until the person's personality (soul) is absorbed into Brahma. This is the sought-for outcome of death. Brahma is the only reality, while the physical universe is a mere illusion. But before reaching Brahma, they must face the horrifying prospect of thousands of re-births and deaths.

No, reincarnation is not a reality and is not taught in the Bible. The Bible clearly refutes reincarnation. Hebrews 9:27 says, "Just as man is destined to die once, and after that to face judgment." God has appointed man to die once and then he will face judgment for this one life that he lived. This is why we are told not to put off salvation: "Today if you hear His voice, do not harden your hearts" (Hebrews 3: 7; 15; 4:7).

I was told that the rapture of the Church is imminent – that there are no signs to be fulfilled before it takes place and that it can happen anytime. Where is this found in the Scriptures? Please explain.

This is true. The rapture of the living believers and the resurrection of those believers who have died in the Lord can take place at any time. All we are told is that it is the next event for the believer in Christ. The believer's eternal destiny is to *be with the Lord forever*, either when we pass on or when the rapture takes place, whichever one comes first. If the rapture takes place first, those who are alive during that time will be glorified without experiencing death.

The Scripture where this is found is 1 Corinthians 15:20-23: "But Christ has indeed been raised from the dead, the first-fruits of those who have fallen asleep. For since death came through a man, the resurrection of the dead comes through a man. For as in Adam all die, so in Christ all will be made alive. But each in his own turn: Christ, the first-fruits; then when he comes, those who belong to Him."

Here the Scripture tells us the order of the first resurrection: "But each in his own turn: Christ, the first-fruits; then when He comes, those who belong to Him."

We are told that Christ is the first-fruits of the resurrection, after this would come those who belong to Him, meaning all believers. In verse 23 we are told that Christ, the first-fruits, has already been raised. This would be followed by those "who belong to Him."

Since the order of the resurrection has already begun and Christ, the first-fruits, has already been raised from the dead, the next event on the agenda in the order of the first resurrection is "when He comes, those who belong to Him." This will take place before the tribulation begins.

Will the Church go through the tribulation?

No. The tribulation is the beginning of the "Day of the Lord." We are told in Zephaniah 1:14-18 that the "day of the Lord" is a "day of darkness and gloom, a day of clouds and blackness."

Joel 2:1-3 tells us the same thing. It will be a "day of darkness and gloom, a day of clouds and blackness."

1 Thessalonians 5:1-11 tells believers that they do not have to fear this day of darkness when "destruction will come upon them suddenly." They are also told, "But you, brothers and sisters, are not in darkness, so that this day should surprise you like a thief. You are all sons of light and sons of the day. We do not belong to the night or to the darkness as unbelievers do (darkness is their natural element)." He goes on to tell them that believers who are of the day should not be like unbelievers who are asleep They are not of the night and darkness when people get drunk and sleep.

Believers should be the opposite of those in darkness and be self-controlled and put on the "hope of salvation as a helmet. For God did not appoint us to suffer wrath (of the great tribulation) but to receive salvation (at the rapture) through our Lord Jesus Christ." Paul reminds us, "He died for us so that, whether we are awake (alive) or asleep (in death), we may live together with Him (at the rapture)."

We are told here that the tribulation is a period of darkness and wrath and is for the children of darkness. But believers are children of light and sons of the day and should not sleep or be drunk like unbelievers but watch for the Lord to come for us and rescue us from the darkness of the tribulation period.

Please explain Daniel's 70 weeks.

This is found in Daniel 9:24-27: "Seventy 'sevens' are decreed for your people and your holy city to finish transgression, to put an end to sin, to atone for wickedness, to bring in everlasting righteousness, to seal up vision and prophecy and to anoint the Most Holy Place.

"Know and understand this: from the issuing of the decree to restore and rebuild Jerusalem until the Anointed One, the ruler, comes, there will be seven 'sevens,' and sixty-two 'sevens.' It will be rebuilt with streets and a trench but in times of trouble.

"After the sixty-two 'sevens,' the Anointed One will be cut off and will have nothing. The people of the ruler who will come will destroy the city and the sanctuary. The end will come like a flood: War will continue until the end, and desolations have been decreed.

"He will confirm a covenant with many for one 'seven.' In the middle of the 'seven' he will put an end to sacrifice and offering. And on the wing of the temple, he will set up an abomination that causes desolation, until the end that is decreed is poured out on him."

We must first understand that this prophecy has to do with the Jewish people and the city of Jerusalem; that is, Daniel's people and their holy city of Jerusalem.

"Seventy sevens" means seventy units; here it means "seventy weeks," which means week of years. Israel had a calendar week of seven days: "Six days do your work, but on the seventh day do not work" (Exodus 23:12). And also a week of seven years: "For six years sow your fields, and for six years prune your vineyards and gather your crops. But in the seventh year, the land is to have a Sabbath of rest, a Sabbath to the Lord" (Leviticus 25:3-4).

This is made clear in Scripture. In Genesis 29:26-28 we read, "Laban replied, 'It is not our custom here to give our younger daughter in marriage before the older one. Finish this daughter's bridal week; then we will give you the younger one also, in return for another seven years of work.' And Jacob did so. He finished the week with Leah, and then Laban gave him his daughter Rachel to be his wife."

This is seen in the seventy-year captivity that was the result of Israel's disobedience. They were to allow the land to remain idle every seventh year. But they disobeyed. After 490 years, they had failed to keep 70 yearly Sabbaths, which led to 70 years of captivity: "The land enjoyed its Sabbath rests; all the time of its desolation it rested until the seventy years were completed in fulfillment of the word spoken by Jeremiah" (2 Chronicles 36:21).

Daniel would have been familiar with the "week of years" because of the seventy years of captivity that Israel was going through at the time. Around 600 B.C., Daniel himself was taken as one of the captives to Babylon. Daniel would have understood when he was told that it would be another period similar in length to the Babylonian exile.

This is the context that led to the 70-year Babylonian captivity. Israel had not kept the yearly Sabbaths for 490 years, which would equal 70 Sabbaths they had to make up for – thus the 70-year captivity.

This means that there were 490 years (70 years times 7 weeks) decreed for Daniel's people. It must be kept in mind that these years are Jewish in context and are 360 days each rather than our year of 365 days.

Daniel 9:24 goes on to list six things that will be accomplished during this period concerning God's program for Israel ("For your people and your holy city").

1. Finish the transgression.

2. Make an end of sin.

3. Make reconciliation for iniquity.

4. Bring in everlasting righteousness.

5. Seal up vision and prophesy.

6. Anoint the Most Holy.

These last three will be fulfilled at Christ's second coming.

In verses 25-26 we are told that from the issuing of the decree to restore and rebuild Jerusalem until the Anointed One (Messiah) was to be 69 weeks (7 plus 62 sevens or 483 years). The decree to restore and rebuild Jerusalem was given by Artaxerxes Longimanus who commissioned Ezra to return to Jerusalem in 457 B.C. (Ezra 7:11-26). He commanded the rebuilding of Jerusalem in 445 B.C.

Using the Jewish year of 360 days, we can determine the exact time of the Messiah, the Anointed One. We can therefore determine the total amount of days in 69 weeks – 69 weeks of years total 483 years. Then multiply this number by 360 days for each year. This totals exactly 173,880 days until the coming Anointed Messiah. This brings us to Passover on April 6, 32 A.D., the day Jesus rode into Jerusalem on a donkey.

Five hundred years before the birth of Christ, the prophet Zechariah wrote that the Messiah, the king, would make Himself known to Israel by riding into Jerusalem on a donkey: "Rejoice greatly, O Daughter of Zion! Shout, Daughter of Jerusalem! See, your King comes to you riding on a donkey, on a colt, the foal of a donkey" (9:9).

Today this is known as Palm Sunday. Jesus rode into Jerusalem on a donkey. Donkeys were ridden by kings of Israel. Jesus was publicly presenting Himself as the Messiah, with full knowledge that this would lead Him to the cross. The crowd shouted: "Blessed be the Son of David! Blessed is He who comes in the name of the Lord. Hosanna in the highest" (Matthew 21:9).

Hosanna means *save now*, while the terms "Son of David" and "He who comes in the name of the Lord" were both strong Messianic terms. This was a Jewish royal entry.

Luke 19:41-44 tells us, "As He approached Jerusalem and saw the city, He wept over it and said, 'If you, even you, had only known on this day what would bring you peace – but now it is hidden from your eyes.'" Then He went on to predict the destruction of Jerusalem: "They will not leave one stone upon another, because you did not recognize the time of God's coming to you." Here He refers to the destruction of Jerusalem in 70 A.D., about 40 years after His crucifixion.

Daniel 9:26 states that after 69 weeks, the Messiah would be "cut off" or killed. This ties in with the preceding part of the prophecy concerning the "making reconciliation for iniquity." That sin must be dealt with is the underlying reason for his being "cut off." He was cut off for the sins of the world (Isaiah 53: 5-6).

Then we are told in Daniel 9:26, "The people of the ruler who will come will destroy the city and the sanctuary." This happened 43 years later when the Romans destroyed Jerusalem and the temple in putting down the Jewish revolt in 70 A.D.

The point of Daniel's prophecy is that 490 years were determined to deal with the question of sin by the Messiah, who would be "cut off" (killed violently) after which Jerusalem and the temple would be destroyed (70 A.D.). And the Jewish people were driven among the nations.

After the 69th week, an interval between the 69th and 70th weeks of Israel's history began while Israel was out of the land. The seventy "sevens" that were determined on Daniel's people were interrupted after the 69th "seven" while Israel was out of the land and set aside in God's dealings. And God began dealing with the Church, which began at Pentecost and will last until the completion of the Church age; that is, the rapture of the Church. Then God will again take up His dealings with Israel and complete the 70th "seven" which is also known as the tribulation period.

God is now working through the Church until the Church is taken out at the rapture. Then God will begin again dealing with Israel during the tribulation period ("a time of trouble for Jacob") which will culminate at Christ's return to rescue Israel.

When the Bible describes hell as eternal, doesn't the word eternal simply mean "ages unto ages," meaning it will end?

The word "eternal" does mean "ages unto the ages," but this does not mean it will end. In the Biblical usage, the term in both Hebrew and Greek always refers to endless time, or unending ages. In the Greek the plural is used, "unto the ages of the ages," to refer to the unending ages of eternity (See Ephesians 2:7, 3:21).

God as "King of ages" refers to God as "the King of unending ages" or the "Eternal" or "Everlasting King" and refers to His dominion over all – past, present, and future time. So when hell is said to be unto the "ages of the ages," it refers to "unending" time.

Who will be raptured? Is there a partial rapture? And what does Paul mean by the "mystery" of 1 Corinthians 15:51?

Concerning the rapture of believers, we read in 1 Corinthians 15:51-52, "Listen, I will tell you a mystery: We will not all sleep, but we will all be changed – in a flash, in the twinkling of an eye, at the last trumpet."

A *mystery* is a truth not fully revealed in the Old Testament but now fully revealed in the New Testament. The fact that all believers will be changed at the resurrection of the just is revealed in the Old Testament in such passages as Psalm 17:15: As for me, I will be vindicated and will see your face; when I awake, I will be satisfied with seeing your likeness."

But what has not been revealed in the Old Testament is the truth that not all believers will die in order to experience this change. The generation that lives to see the rapture will be changed instantly. But now notice that while not all believers will die, all believers will be changed at the rapture. The rapture and resurrection are not a reward but part of the believer's salvation.

All believers form the body of Christ and cannot be divided: "The body is a unit, though it is made up of many parts, and though all its parts are many, they form one body, so it is with Christ" (I Corinthians 12:12). The rapture is a part of our salvation, not a reward. Rewards will be given out at the judgment seat of Christ which will follow the rapture.

How can the rapture be imminent? Doesn't the Gospel have to be preached to the whole world first (Matthew 24:14)?

Matthew 24:14 says, "And this gospel of the kingdom will be preached in the whole world as a testimony to all nations, and then the end will come."

I think you are confusing the rapture with the second coming. The rapture is imminent. The preaching of the gospel will be done by Israel during the tribulation period after the rapture of believers. This is recorded in Revelation Chapter 7 with the sealing of the 144, 000 saved Jews: "Then I saw another angel coming up from the east, having the seal of the living God. He called out in a loud voice to the four angels who had been given power to harm the land and the sea: 'do not harm the land or the sea or the trees until we put a seal on the foreheads of the servants or our God.' Then I heard the number of those who were sealed: 144,000 from all the tribes of Israel" (verses 2-4).

The result of this sealing is recorded in verses 9-10: "After this, I looked and there before me was a great multitude that no one could count from every nation, tribe, people and language standing before the throne and in front of the Lamb. They were wearing white robes and were holding palm branches in their hands, and they cried out in a loud voice: 'Salvation belongs to our God, who sits on the throne and to the Lamb.'"

Then in verses 13 and 14 we read: "Then one of the elders asked me, these in white robes – who are they, and where do they come from?'

"I answered, 'Sir, you know.'

"And he said, 'these are they who have come out of the great tribulation; they have washed their robes and made them white in the blood of the Lamb.'"

The "end" referred to in Matthew 24:14 is not the rapture but the Second Coming of Christ in judgment.

Does the judgment referred to in Romans 14:10-12 apply to Christians? Didn't Christ take our judgment on the cross? Why then are we still judged?

The word "judgment seat" in Romans 14:10 is literally *bema*, which refers to the elevated seat on which the judge of the Olympic contests sat. After the contests were over, the winners would assemble before the bema to receive their rewards or crowns of laurel leaves. Those who did not win or were disqualified received no rewards. It was not a judicial seat but only for rewards. Christ has already been judged for our sins. This is a judgment put into effect after we receive Christ. But eternal security does not allow believers to live any way they please. What believers do in this life has eternal repercussions.

We must understand the difference between salvation and rewards. Salvation cannot be earned by good works but is something that Christ alone can provide through faith. Rewards, on the other hand, are earned after we have received salvation as a free gift provided by Christ through His death on the cross.

Believers are both sons and servants. When we are saved, we become sons through faith in Christ; it is something that Christ earned for us and we receive by faith. On the other hand, rewards are through good works and are earned: "Do you not know that in a race all the runners run, but only one gets the prize? Run in such a way as to get the prize. Everyone who competes in the games goes into strict training. They do it to get a crown that will not last; but we do it to get a crown that will last forever. Therefore I do not run like a man running aimlessly; I do not fight like a man beating the air. No, I beat my body and make it my slave so that after I have preached to others, I myself will not be disqualified for the prize" (1 Corinthians 9: 24-27).

In verse 24, we are told that like athletes we must have a single mind on the goal line, determined to win.

In verse 25, it is shown that athletes must have self-control and discipline themselves by self-denial and hard work. Their goal is a mere crown of laurel-leaves that will fade away along with their earthly fame. But we will receive eternal crowns.

In verse 26, Paul tells us that he ran his race deliberately, without uncertainty. He knew where the goal line was; he pressed toward it with all his might. When he boxed, he did not merely beat the air but landed his blows where they counted, going for the knockout.

In verse 27, Paul says he keeps himself well conditioned so that after training others to run the race, he himself is not disqualified from receiving the reward.

In 1 Corinthians 3:10-15, the believer's life is compared to a building: "By the grace God has given me, I laid a foundation as an expert builder, and someone else is building upon it. But each one should be careful how he builds. For no one can lay any foundation other than the one already laid, which is Jesus Christ. If any man builds on this foundation using gold, silver, costly stones, wood, hay or straw, his work will be shown for what it is, because the day will bring it to light. It will be revealed with fire, and the fire will test the quality of each man's work. If what he has built survives, he will receive his reward. If it is burned up, he will suffer loss; he himself will be saved, but only as one escaping through the flames."

Here in verses 10 and 11, the foundation of the believer's life is Christ. There is no other foundation for the believer. All those on any other foundation will not appear at this judgment for believers but rather at the great white throne judgment for the unsaved. By faith in Christ, the believer rests eternally on the Foundation of Christ. This constitutes salvation. After salvation, the believer is to build on this foundation.

In verse 12, there are two categories of building materials – things that will burn (wood, hay, and stubble) and things that will not burn (gold, silver, and precious stones). In verse 13, the quality of the believer's works will be made manifest on that day because it will be tested by fire.

In verses 14-15, the works that are acceptable to God will not burn and will receive a reward. Those whose works are burned up will receive no reward, but they themselves will be saved because they are on the true foundation of Jesus Christ. Those who receive no rewards will be saved "as one escaping through the flames."

This is a figure of a person who is asleep and wakes up and finds the house is on fire. The flames and smoke are so bad that all he can do is leap out the window to safety, while his loved ones and all their possessions will be lost. This is a picture of believers who accomplish nothing for the Lord. They don't even win their own loved ones to the lord. They themselves will be saved but all else will be lost, leaving them with shame and remorse.

Every believer is on equal ground when it comes to receiving rewards. Some have greater opportunities and abilities than others. But it is faithfulness with what we do have that counts. "Now it is required that those who have been given a trust must be faithful" (I Corinthians 4:2).

Serving the Lord brings rewards now in the peace and joy in knowing we are serving the Lord, but most of these rewards are coming later. Serving God is often a thankless job and many are tempted to give up. But we are encouraged by the Word of God: "Let us not become weary in doing good, for at the proper time we will reap a harvest if we do not give up" (Galatians 6: 9).

1 Corinthians 15:58 exhorts us: "Therefore, my dear brothers, stand firm, let nothing move you. Always give yourselves fully to the work of the Lord, because you know that your labor in the Lord is not in vain." The smallest reward at this judgment will be worth more than all this world.

Could you please explain the false prophet? Who is He? Is he a Jew? Is he the Antichrist?

He is not the Antichrist. The Antichrist is seen in Revelation 13:1-8: "And I saw a beast coming up out of the sea. And he had ten horns and seven heads, with ten crowns on his horns, and on each head a blasphemous name. The beast I saw resembled a leopard but had feet like those of a bear and a mouth like that of a lion. The dragon gave the beast his power and his throne and great authority. One of the heads of the beast seemed to have had a fatal wound, but the fatal wound had been healed. The whole world was astonished and followed the beast. Men worshipped the dragon because he had given authority to the beast, and they also worshipped the beast and asked, 'who is like the beast? Who can make war against him?'

"The beast was given a mouth to utter proud words and blasphemies and to exercise his authority for forty-two months. He opened his mouth to blaspheme God, and to slander His name and His dwelling place and those who live in heaven. He was given power to make war against the saints and to conquer them. And he was given authority over every tribe, people, language, and nation. All the inhabitants of the earth will worship the beast – all whose names have not been written in the book of life belonging to the Lamb that was slain from the creation of the world" (Revelation 13:1-8).

Here we have a reference to the revived Roman Empire described in the Book of Daniel 7:7-8: "After that, in my vision at night I looked, and there before me was a fourth beast – terrifying and frightening and very powerful. It had large iron teeth; it crushed and devoured its victims and trampled underfoot whatever was left. It was different from all the other former beasts, and it had ten horns.

"While I was thinking about the horns, there before me was another horn, a little one, which came up among them; and three of the first horns were uprooted before it. This horn had eyes like the eyes of a man and a mouth that spoke boastfully."

This describes the Empire as it will appear during the great tribulation, after the rise of the little horn, who breaks off three of the horns (nations). (Daniel 7:8).

Revelation 13:2 tells us that the Antichrist will receive his power and throne and great authority from the dragon (Satan).

Revelation 13:11-18 describes the false prophet and his work: "Then I saw another beast, coming out of the earth. He had two horns like a lamb, but he spoke like a dragon. He exercised all the authority of the first beast on his behalf, and made the earth and its inhabitants worship the first beast, whose fatal wound had been healed. And he performed great and miraculous signs, even causing fire to come down from heaven to earth in full view of men. Because of the signs he was given power to do on behalf of the first beast, he deceived the inhabitants of the earth. He ordered them to set up an image in honor of the beast who was wounded by the sword yet lived. He was given power to give breath to the image of the first beast, so that it could speak and caused all who refused to worship the image to be killed. He also forced everyone, small and great, rich and poor, free and slave, to receive a mark on his right hand or on his forehead, so that no one could buy or sell unless he had the mark, which is the name of the beast or the number of his name. This calls for wisdom. If anyone has insight, let him calculate the number of the beast, for it is man's number. His number is 666."

All dictators have ministers of propaganda. Hitler had Joseph Goebbels who led mass rallies for Hitler as Germany's savior and god. Hymns were changed to honor Hitler, etc. All the Caesars were worshipped as divine. In verse 11, the false prophet is described as appearing like a minister of peace, but his doctrine will be Satanic.

It seems obvious that he will not be Jewish since that will be one of the groups he will persecute along with Christians.

4. Questions About the Bible

Who wrote the Bible? I heard Dave Hunt say God is the author of the Bible, but later he says human writers wrote the various books of the Bible. This is confusing. Either God wrote the Bible or humans did. How can you have it both ways?

Actually, Dave Hunt was correct in both statements. God is the Author of the Bible, while men were the penmen who wrote the words. The Bible is a revelation from God. This means that God has made Himself known to mankind, who otherwise could not have known Him.

We are told in 1 Corinthians 1:21, "The world through its wisdom did not know Him." And in I Corinthians 2:9-10 we read, "However, as it is written: 'No eye has seen, no ear has heard, no mind has conceived what God has prepared for those who love Him' – but God has revealed it to us by His Spirit." Thus, we could know nothing about God other than what He has been pleased to reveal to us.

2 Timothy 3:16 says, "All Scripture is God-breathed." This is the result of the creative breath of God. In Scripture, the breath of God is a symbol of His Almighty creative power. For example, Psalm 33:6 says, "By the word of the Lord were the heavens made, their starry host by the breath of His mouth." God's breath is the irresistible outflow of His power. The Holy Spirit is often identified with the breath of God. After

His resurrection, Jesus appeared to His disciples and we read, "Again Jesus said, 'peace be with you! As the Father has sent me, I am sending you.' And with that He breathed on them and said, 'Receive the Holy Spirit'" (John 20:21-22).

That the Scriptures have their origin in God rather than the writers themselves is clearly brought out in I Peter 1:10-12: "Concerning this salvation, the prophets who spoke of the grace that was to come unto you, searched intently with the greatest care, trying to find out the time and circumstances to which the Spirit of Christ in them was pointing when he predicted the sufferings of Christ and the glories that would follow. It was revealed to them that they were not serving themselves but you, when they spoke of the things that have now been told you by those who have preached the gospel to you by the Holy Spirit sent from heaven. Even angels long to look into these things."

Here we are told that many times the writers of the Bible did not understand what they wrote. These Old Testament prophets had to study their own manuscripts to learn what they meant, because it was "the Spirit of Christ" (that is, the Holy Spirit) which was in them that told them of the future sufferings of Christ and the glory that should follow. And they understood that what God gave them to write down referred to a later time after Christ came.

"Above all, you must understand that no prophecy of Scripture came about by the prophet's own interpretation. For prophecy never had its origin in the will of man, but men spoke from God as they were carried along by the Holy Spirit" (2 Peter 1:20-21).

Here the word "prophecy" does not merely refer to telling future events, but to all the words given by God. We are told that no Scripture came about by the will of man but that God spoke through them while they were "carried along by the Holy Spirit." They were "carried along" like a ship with its sails in the wind. They were passive in the origin of the message and were active in relating or writing down the message.

The writers were like the pen in God's hand. Their intelligence, vocabulary and style, etc. were under Divine control so that what was written was Authored by God. When writing something other than Scripture, the writers were as fallible as any other men.

God's control goes even further. God prepared the human writers even before they were conceived in the womb. An example of this is the prophet Jeremiah: "The word of the Lord came to me, saying 'before I formed you in the womb I knew you, before you were born I set you apart; I appointed you as a prophet to the nations'" (Jeremiah 1:4-5).

The same can be said about Paul: "But when God, who set me apart from birth and called me by His grace, was pleased to reveal His Son in me so that I might preach Him among the Gentiles." (Galatians 1:15-16).

How did Noah fit the millions and millions of species on this planet into his ark?

First of all, experts in this area say there are no more than 18,000 species. How big was the ark? The dimensions given are 300 cubits long, 50 cubits wide, and 30 cubits high. To calculate this, we must know the length of a cubit. The cubit was of varying lengths in the ancient world. But to be safe we will take the shortest cubit, which was 17.5 inches. In that case the ark would have been 438 feet long and 72.9 feet wide and 43.8 feet high.

It had three platforms or decks 10 cubits high that were to be divided into rooms or stalls (*nests* in Hebrew) meaning each stall was to be the appropriate size for each animal to inhabit.

The holding capacity of the ark was about 1,400,000 cubic feet, which is equal to the holding capacity of 522 standard boxcars for livestock as used on modern American railroads. The average animal is about the size of a sheep. Large animals such as dinosaurs and elephants and other very large animals would have been young and much smaller. Some 240 sheep can be transported comfortably in one stock car; 125,000 sheep could have been carried on the ark.

It was to be made waterproof by covering it with pitch inside and outside. The window or opening was to be one cubit from the roof running all around the circumference of the ark for light and ventilation and for gathering rainwater for drinking and washing.

As the flood neared, God sent the animals to the ark: "Noah was six hundred years old when the flood waters came on the earth. And Noah and his sons and his wife and his sons' wives entered the ark to escape the waters of the flood. Pairs of clean and unclean animals, of birds and of all creatures that move along the ground, male and female, came to Noah and entered the ark, as God had commanded Noah."

At the proper time, God brought the animals to Noah, and Noah placed them in the ark in their proper places. And as a built-in protection against extreme weather and other severe climate changes, God gave animals the ability to hibernate, thereby suspending all bodily functions, so they could pass winter in confined areas.

Is the Bible inerrant?

Inerrancy means true and without error. In John 10:35, Jesus said, "The Scripture cannot be broken" or lie. In Matthew 5:18, He said, "I tell you the truth, until heaven and earth disappear, not the smallest letter, not the least stroke of a pen, will by any means disappear from the Law until everything is accomplished."

Jesus said it came from "the mouth of God" (Matthew 4:4). And in 2 Timothy 3:16 Paul wrote "all Scripture is God-breathed" or inspired by God. God breathed out the words and prepared men to record them. "Above all, you must understand that no prophecy of Scripture came about by the prophet's own interpretation. For prophecy never had its origin in the will of man, but men spoke from God as they were carried along by the Holy Spirit" (2 Peter 1: 20-21).

The words "carried along" have the meaning of "being driven," like a sailboat driven or overpowered by the wind. The writers were overpowered or controlled by the Holy Spirit. They were the penmen but God was the Author, and they wrote what He wanted written.

Who was Cain's wife?

After Cain killed his brother Abel (Genesis 4:8), God's punishment was to send him away from his home and from God's presence. We are told that Cain was afraid that he would be killed by someone seeking revenge (Genesis 4:14) and that he lay with his wife and she became pregnant and gave birth to a son (Genesis 4:17) and that he even built a city.

The question must be asked not only who was Cain's wife but also where did all these other people come from? These would have been his brothers and sisters or even his children. When we consider the life span of the human race at that time was 912 years, we see that the population would have been rather large.

When Adam was 130 years old, Seth was born in place of the murdered Abel (Genesis 5:3). Then we are told that after the birth of

Seth, Adam lived another 800 years and had other sons and daughters (Genesis 5:3).

Adam's sons and daughters were also giving birth to sons and daughters. At that time of the first generation of mankind, all marriages would have been between brothers and sisters. The Bible does not indicate the age of Cain when he killed Abel or took a wife or built this city, so there would have been plenty of time for the population to grow immensely during Cain's lifetime.

Such a relationship between brother and sister would eventually be forbidden by Mosaic Law. But at this beginning point of human development, it would not have been unnatural or wrong. In later generations, such relationships would be understood as harmful genetically and forbidden as incest. However, at that early period, there would have been no harmful mutant genes. It would not have been until many generations later, until the time of Moses, that enough mutations would have accumulated to make such unions genetically dangerous.

What does it mean that God hardened Pharaoh's heart? Does God deliberately harden some hearts so they will not believe?

First of all, it must be understood that the issue between God and Pharaoh was not salvation but letting Israel go out of Egyptian bondage. God confronted Pharaoh and forced the issue, and Pharaoh's heart was hardened.

Pharaoh had already hardened his heart (Exodus 8:15; 9:34) and murdered Hebrew babies, cruelly treated God's people, and resisted God's command to release His people from bondage. When Pharaoh was set in his determination, God pressed the issue by sending the ten plagues. There is no doubt that Pharaoh was unsaved but that was his own choice. But the question of Pharaoh's salvation is not the issue here.

The Scriptures are very clear that God loves mankind and that "He is patient with you, not wanting anyone to perish, but everyone to come to repentance" (2 Peter 3:9). Christ's suffering and death on the cross was God's love letter to all mankind, written in Christ's blood.

What does the Bible say about Dinosaurs? Are there dinosaurs in the Bible?

I believe dinosaurs are referred to in the Bible. However, it was not until 1841 that Sir Richard Owen of the British museum coined the term "dinosaur" from two Greek words meaning *terrible lizard*. So we will not find the term in the Bible. However, the term *dragon* is found 30 times in the Old Testament.

There are also many dragon legends from around the world. The descriptions of these creatures are remarkably like dinosaurs. Genesis 1:21 tells us, "So God created the great creatures of the sea." Here the Hebrew word for "great creatures" is *tannin*, translated in other places as *dragon*. Down through the ages, we find accounts of dragons in many countries of the world.

In Job 40: 15-19, we read of behemoth, which means *great beast*: "Look at behemoth, which I made along with you and which feeds on grass like an ox. What strength he has in his loins, what power in the muscles of his belly! His tail sways like a cedar; the sinews of his thighs are close-knit. His bones are tubes of bronze, his limbs like rods of iron, he ranks first among the works of God."

Chapter 41 of Job describes leviathan, meaning *sea serpent* or *sea monster* as a creature that lived in the sea and breathed fire. In Isaiah 27:1, we read of "Leviathan the gliding serpent, Leviathan the coiling serpent."

The Biblical descriptions of both behemoth and leviathan defy any living animals and seem to clearly refer to something now extinct: behemoth to a land-dwelling dinosaur and leviathan to a sea-dwelling dinosaur. Only this seems to make any real sense of the descriptions given.

Please explain Exodus 34:14. Isn't it petty for God to be jealous?

This verse of Scripture reads, "Do not worship any other god, for the Lord, whose name is Jealous, is a jealous God."

It would definitely be a mistake to equate the jealousy of a holy and loving God to that of fallen sinful mankind. The word translated as *jealous* is the Hebrew word *qanna* which could also be translated as *zealous*. God is zealous that mankind makes Him the goal of all their desires and longings. The Scriptures present God and His people in a husband-wife relationship or in a father-child relationship.

It is natural and right for a husband to want his wife to be faithful to him. This type of jealousy is a good thing. God expects all of our love because we have all of His love as revealed in His crucifixion. He insists upon top priority in our lives and that we love Him with all our heart, soul, and strength (Deuteronomy 6:4).

He is jealous for our benefit, and He knows that only He can fulfill all our needs and desires. It is not a selfish jealousy but a self-giving jealousy. It's the same jealousy that causes a father to say to his child, "I am your father and you must never call another man Father. I have a relationship to you that no one else has, and you cannot trust another to care for you like I do."

What is the significance of manna in the Bible?

In the Old Testament, in the Book of Exodus, when Israel was wandering in the desert, God fed them manna from heaven. "Moses said to them, 'It is the bread the Lord has given you to eat.'" (Exodus 16:14-15). God also gave them water from a rock: "The Lord answered Moses, 'Walk on ahead of the people. Take with you some of the elders of Israel and take in your hand the staff with which you struck the Nile, and go. I will stand there before you by the rock at Horeb. Strike the rock, and water will come out of it for the people to drink'" (Exodus 17:6).

These were symbols of the True Bread from heaven and the Water of Life. In John 6:30-31 the people asked Jesus, "What miraculous sign then will you give that we may see it and believe you? What will you do? Our fathers ate the manna in the desert; as it is written: He gave them bread from heaven to eat."

Jesus tells them that this was only a figure or illustration of the true bread from heaven. "Jesus said to them, 'I tell you the truth, it is not Moses who has given you the bread from heaven, but it is my Father who gives you the true bread from heaven. For the bread of God is he who comes down from heaven and gives his life to the world.'"

But they didn't understand the spiritual significance of what He was saying and thought he was talking about physical bread. "'Sir,' they said, 'from now on give us this bread.'" Then Jesus made it very clear to them: "I am the bread of life, he who comes to me will never go hungry, and he who believes in me will never be thirsty" (verses 32-35).

In verses 47-51 Jesus continues, "I tell you the truth, he who believes in me has everlasting life. I am the bread of life. Your forefathers ate the manna in the desert, yet they died. But here is the bread that comes down from heaven, which a man may eat and not die. I am the living bread that came down from heaven. If anyone eats of this bread, he will live forever. This bread is my flesh, which I will give for the life of the world."

1 Corinthians 10:3-4 gives added details of this truth about the spiritual meaning of the manna and the water that came out of the rock: "They all ate the same spiritual food and drank the same spiritual drink; for they drank from the spiritual rock that accompanied them, and that rock was Christ (a symbol of Christ)."

Does the Bible teach the doctrine of original sin?

Yes, the Bible very vividly teaches the doctrine of original sin. The fall of Adam and Eve was a definite event that occurred in human history. Mankind's tragic sin and fall is not a mythological story of something that happened a long time ago. It is a reality that is going on today in the life of every human being. The Biblical record in Genesis 3 is the truth that lies behind every sin being committed today. Original sin was, first of all, the questioning of whether or not God has spoken and given a revelation of Himself: "Did God really say?" (verse 1). In other words, is the Bible really the word of God?

Then there is the open denial of God's Word: "You will not surely die" (verse 4).

Then there is the appeal to pride: "You will be like God" (verse 4). In effect, Satan was telling them that they didn't need to obey God. They could be their own God and do whatever they wanted.

Then there is actual disobedience: "She took some and ate it."

Thus, the universality of sin entered into the human race.

This transmission of sin into the human race is called "original sin." It is the root sickness of the human race introduced at the conception of every man and woman, which makes all mankind guilty and polluted at the time of birth. Romans 5:12-19 stresses the all-inclusiveness of sin introduced through the headship of Adam over the world, under which all mankind now lives and struggles. It is called *Total Depravity*.

This does not mean that mankind is as bad as they can be, or that they can do nothing good. It means that mankind cannot reach God but that God must reach mankind through a Mediator. It means that we have no access to God but must cling to the means of salvation through Christ. Every obstacle presented by original sin and man's total depravity is demolished through the Mediator provided by God, as we are told in Romans 5:20-21: "But where sin increased, grace increased all the more. So that, just as sin reigned in death, so grace also might reign through righteousness to bring eternal life through Jesus Christ our Lord."

This great truth is reiterated in 1 Corinthians 15: 22: "For as in Adam all die, so in Christ all will be made alive."

I have read the book of Job trying to find why the righteous suffer but always seem to miss it.

Many think the Book of Job explains why the righteous suffer, but it does not. The purpose of the Book of Job is not to tell us why the righteous suffer, but that we are to trust God in the midst of suffering: "Though He slay me, yet will I hope in Him" (Job 13:15).

Who changed the Sabbath from Saturday to Sunday and on what authority?

The Sabbath was not changed to Sunday. The Sabbath was fulfilled in Christ and abolished. The Sabbath was part of the old system under the law which was abolished by Christ, as we are told in Ephesians 2:15: "By abolishing in His flesh the law with its commandments and regulations."

And in Colossians 2:16-17: "Therefore do not let anyone judge you by what you eat or drink, or with regard to a religious festival, a new moon celebration or a Sabbath day. These are a shadow of the things that were to come; the reality however is found in Christ."

We are no longer under the ceremonial laws but under grace (Romans 6:14). The Sabbath honored God as Creator, while *The Lord's Day*, the first day of the week, recognizes the resurrection of Jesus Christ on that day (John 20:1-25) and honors God as Savior. The Seventh Day Adventists claim that there is no basis in Scripture for this change and that the Roman Catholic church or the pope was responsible for the change.

This is not true, however, for Scripture clearly shows that the early church kept the first day of the week from the beginning, before there was a Roman Catholic church. The disciples met on the first day of the week to break bread (Acts 20:7). It was also the day that Pentecost came (Acts 2:1-41).

What does the Bible teach about the Trinity?

The Bible's teaching on the Triune nature of God runs all through the Scriptures. In fact, it is ingrained in the Bible. The following is taken from my book, *The Bible Explained*:

The Bible emphasizes that there is one God. *The Lord our God, the Lord is One* (Deut 6:4).

The Lord Himself is God: besides Him there is no other (Deut 4:35).

I am the first, and I am the last, apart from me there is no God (Isa 44:6).

I am the Lord, and there is no other; apart from me there is no God (Isa 45:5).

However, it is also taught that this one God consists of a plurality of Persons. God is a plurality of one. This sounds strange, but it is what the Bible repeatedly teaches. This is taught in the very Scriptures that emphasize that there is One God. For instance, Deuteronomy 6:4 uses two Hebrew words to emphasize this: *The Lord* (Jehovah—singular), *our God* (Elohim—plural) *is one Lord* (Jehovah—singular).

Deuteronomy 4:35 reads: *The Lord* (Jehovah—singular), *Himself is God* (Elohim—plural)*; there is none other besides Me.*

Isaiah 45:5 reads: *I am the Lord* (Jehovah—singular), *there is no God* (Elohim—plural) *besides Me.*

If the Bible wanted to teach a single entity within the Godhead, the word "Eloah" would have been used instead of the plural "Elohim."

Note in Genesis 1:26: *God said, "Let US make man in OUR image, in OUR likeness.* In the next verse, we read: *So God created man in HIS own image.* The "US" and "OUR" in verse 26, become "HIS" in verse 27. This singular God consists of a plurality of Persons. This singular God with a plurality of Persons also runs all through the New Testament. Note in John 1:1 we have *In the beginning was the Word*

(Jesus Christ), *and the Word was WITH God* (plurality) *and the Word WAS God* (singular).

This plurality is consistently revealed as three Persons. Genesis 1:1 says: *In the beginning God* (Elohim—plural) *created the heavens and the earth.* Here the plural is used, a plurality of Persons. This is why we are told that the FATHER created all things: *The Father from whom all things come* (1 Cor 8:6). The Son created all things: *All things were made through Him, and without Him nothing was made that was made* (John 1:3). And the Holy Spirit is the Creator: *The Spirit of God had made me* (Job 33:4).

Likewise, Jesus' resurrection is attributed to the triune God. To the Father: *This Jesus God has raised up* (Acts 2:32). To the Son: *Therefore My Father loves Me, because I lay down my life that I may take it again* (John 10:17). And to the Holy Spirit: *But if the Spirit of Him who raised Jesus from the dead dwells in you, He who raised Christ from the dead will also give life to your mortal bodies through His Spirit who dwells in you* (Rom 8:11).

These three Persons are coeternal and coequal. They are distinct individuals. Each partakes of the full divine essence. The one God is also three Persons, and they are always together and always cooperating. They are inherently one in the fullness of Deity, in which each one lives in and through the others in a union eternally rooted in infinite love. At the center of reality is a relationship within the nature of God.

They relate in a causal order. The Father is the unseen, omnipresent, and omnipotent source of all being, revealed in and through the Son and applied or experienced through the Holy Spirit. The Father is the intelligence or thought behind the action, the Son is the Word that commands and calls it forth, and the Holy Spirit makes in a reality. The Son proceeds from the Father, and the Spirit proceeds from the Son.

This is clearly seen in both creation and salvation. The Father planned the creation; and as the Word, the Son went forth and gave the command, and the Holy Spirit brought it into existence. Concerning salvation, the Father planned it and sent the Son to accomplish it. Then the Son sent the Holy Spirit to apply it and make it real to the believer.

What does the Bible say about…?

Divorce and Remarriage?
From the beginning, God intended marriage to be permanent. However, there is one ground for divorce in the Bible and that is unfaithfulness to the marriage vow: "But I tell you that anyone who divorces his wife, except for marital unfaithfulness, causes her to become an adulteress, and anyone who marries the divorced woman commits adultery" (Matthew 5:32).

Women in ministry?
We read in 1 Timothy 2:11-12, "A woman should learn in quietness and full submission. I do not permit a woman to teach or to have authority over a man; she must be silent." This followed the culture of the time in which Christ lived. Women were put on the back burner, so to speak, and were not to have a position of teaching men and not to expound the Word of God as an authoritative teacher of men.

It is different today. Some churches have only men in positions of pastoring and teaching. Other churches allow women to be pastors and teachers. The first position extends the culture of the time of Jesus to the present day; the second does not.

Women were very prominent in the gospels. They served and waited on the Lord Jesus. Women were the first ones that Jesus appeared to after

His resurrection and were commissioned to bring the news to the men disciples (John 20:17-18; Matthew 28:9-10). The Apostle Paul commends the woman who struggled at his side in the cause of the gospel.

While God loves and honors men and women the same, He has different positions and service for them within the family, and they complement each other. Outside of the family structure, women today are pastors, teachers, prophets and defenders of the Christian faith. In the Old Testament, Deborah was a prophet and a judge. In the present day, Joyce Meyer has her own ministry.

Speaking in tongues?
Speaking in tongues in Acts was speaking in a foreign language for the preaching of the gospel. Acts 2:1-13 defines the meaning of speaking in tongues when "All of them were filled with the Holy Spirit and began to speak in other tongues as the Spirit enabled them."

The Feast of Pentecost was one of the feasts that every Jew was commanded to attend. Jews from all over the Roman Empire speaking many languages went to Jerusalem. When the disciples spoke in tongues, these many nationalities heard them speak the gospel in their own language.

Jesus had told them, "But you will receive power when the Holy Spirit comes upon you, and you will be my witnesses in Jerusalem, and in all Judea and Samaria, and to the ends of the earth" (Acts 1:8).

Acts 2:5-11 describes the nationalities who were there at Pentecost. These people heard the gospel in their own language, which was made possible by speaking in tongues. The promise was that they were to receive power when the Holy Spirit comes on them, empowering them to witness to the gospel. At Pentecost, a problem presented itself in that they received power but the majority of the people could not understand what they were saying so God performed another miracle that enabled them to speak in many languages

When those from these other nations believed, they would then go back to their own nations and present the gospel in their own languages, giving a kick-start to the preaching of the gospel to the whole world, which is the Great Commission.

Today, Pentecostal and Charismatic churches believe that speaking in tongues is a manifestation of the Holy Spirit in the present age. Other churches do not have that emphasis, and some churches discount speaking in tongues all together.

There is room for these different ways of dealing with tongues in the greater church. The problems arise, as they always do, with those who take something to an extreme. For example, when those who speak in tongues believe those who don't aren't saved or are lesser Christians. There is no evidence that Billy Graham ever spoke in tongues, but one would be hard pressed to claim he wasn't a Christian or was an inferior one. The same holds true for C.S. Lewis.

On the other extreme are Christians who believe that those who speak in tongues are crazy fools or tools of the devil. Who are we to believe that we have the market cornered on holiness or doctrine? It is God who defines, not man.

Interracial marriage?

The Bible is silent on interracial marriage. It is not clear what this question is asking. Is it asking if it is forbidden? No, the only marriage forbidden in the Bible is in 2 Corinthians 6:14: "Do not be yoked together with unbelieves" and verse 15 gives the reason, "What does a believer have in common with an unbeliever?" Marriage should consist of a partnership with both pulling in the same direction. An unequal yoke means both pulling in different directions, with different purposes and goals in life.

Sometimes a believer will go against God's direction and marry an unbeliever thinking they can bring them to Christ after they are married. But usually the opposite happens, and believers backslide to get along with their mates and never accomplish God's purpose in their lives.

Marriage according to the Bible is meant to be permanent. Man was intended to be the head of the household while the woman was to be loved and cherished. The man is to love his wife as Christ loved the church and died for her. This means that while he is the head of the relationship, he is accountable to God to love her as Christ loves the church and must be willing to lay his life down for her. Every decision he makes must be for her benefit as well as his (Ephesians 5:22-25). Some men abdicate their role, and it then becomes the role of the wife to raise the children to love God and follow Jesus. One could hardly say that a woman should never do that. Deborah in Judges took charge of the battle when Barak shrunk back from his role as the commanding officer of the Israelites, and God gave her credit for it.

Christian Tithing?

The New Testament does not specifically command tithing as it was under the Law in Old Testament times. In the New Testament, giving was to be done willingly and cheerfully: "Each man should give what he has decided in his heart to give, not reluctantly or under compulsion, for God loves a cheerful giver" (2 Corinthians 9:7). However, we must remember that believers are commissioned to do their share in getting out the gospel "In keeping with his income" (1 Corinthians 16:2).

After His resurrection before His ascension into heaven, Jesus gave His people the Great Commission (Mark 16:15). This commission was not given only to the apostles but to all believers. This is clearly taught in Scripture and is how the early church understood it.

We read in Acts 8:2: "On that day a great persecution broke out against the church at Jerusalem, and all except the apostles were scattered throughout Judea and Samaria." Then verse 4 tells of those who were scattered: "Those who had been scattered preached the Word wherever they went."

So we are all responsible to spread the gospel. Believers are not only responsible for giving, but also where we give. In 2 Corinthians 9: 6, we are exhorted to give generously: "Remember this: Whoever sows sparingly will also reap sparingly and whoever sows generously will also reap generously."

God promises to bless our giving: "And God is able to make all grace abound to you, so that in all things at all times, having all that you need, you will abound in every good work."

Drinking alcohol?
It is important to understand that there are two different kinds of wine in the Bible. It was called wine when it was freshly squeezed grape juice that we read of in Proverbs 3:10: "When your barns are filled to overflowing, and your vats will brim over with new wine."

"New wine" is freshly squeezed grape juice. Then there are many warnings against intoxicating or fermented wine as in Proverbs 23:31-33: "Do not gaze at wine when it is red, when it sparkles in the cup, when it goes down smoothly! In the end it bites like a snake and poisons like a viper. Your eyes will see strange sights and your mind imagine confusing things." The writer is not saying that you shouldn't drink any alcoholic drinks but that you must not drink to the point where you see strange sights and confusing things. Can there be a clearer definition of what it means to be drunk? "Do not get drunk on wine, which leads to debauchery" (Ephesians 5:18). This is another warning not to drink to excess.

There are churches today that forbid their members to drink. Their fear is that no good comes from alcohol. Indeed, there are those who should never have any alcohol to drink because they have addictive personalities and are best off not drinking at all. Other churches accept drinking in moderation. And there are those who believe there is no sin in drinking to excess or drinking in front of those who are perhaps addicted to alcohol and prone to stumble when someone they respect drinks in front of them.

Tattoos?
Is it wrong to have tattoos? That would, of course, depend on the tattoo. A well-placed tattoo saying *Mom* or *Jesus* or *America* etc. would be appropriate. Of course, if you are a Christian, then the rule of thumb would be 1 Corinthians 6:19-20: "Do you not know that your body is a temple of the Holy Spirit, who is in you, whom you have received from God? You are not your own; you were bought at a price. Therefore glorify God with your body."

And 1 Corinthians 10:31: "So whether you eat or drink or whatever you do, do it all for the glory of God."

If we make these two verses rules for our lives, we will not go wrong.

What did Jesus mean when He said, "Do not judge or you will be judged" and "with the measure you use, it will be measured out to you?"

This verse is found in Matthew 7:1. The thought here is that we are not to judge in a self-righteous way that which we would not want to be judged for ourselves. It does not mean that we are to condone each other's sin as if saying, "You condone my sins and I will condone yours."

The chapter goes on to show that we are to exercise discrimination in judging Scripturally (6, 9-11, 13, 15). What is forbidden is a critical attitude of self-righteous superiority, not an honest evaluation of whether or not something is according to Scripture. Some people try to build up their own self-esteem by tearing down others. This is what is forbidden.

Could Jesus have sinned?

Absolutely not! Jesus did take on humanity, but it was sinless, perfect humanity with no sin nature. In John 14:30 Jesus said, as He was about to go to the cross, "I will not speak with you much longer, for the prince of this world is coming. He has no hold on me, but the world must learn that I love the Father and that I do exactly what my Father has commanded me."

Satan has a hold on everyone else through the fallen sin nature, but Christ had no fallen, sinful nature. This is why Jesus could bear our sins and pay our penalty, because He had none of His own. "God made Him, who had no sin, to be sin for us, so that in Him we might become the righteousness of God" (2 Corinthians 6:21). Jesus went to the cross, not because Satan had a hold on Him, but because he had a hold on everyone else.

What was Paul's thorn in the flesh?

In 2 Corinthians 12:7-10 Paul writes, "To keep me from becoming conceited because of these surpassingly great revelations, there was given me a thorn in my flesh, a messenger of Satan, to torment me. Three times I pleaded with the Lord to take it away from me. But He said to me, 'My grace is sufficient for you, for My power is made perfect in weakness.' Therefore, I will boast all the more gladly about my weaknesses, so that Christ's power may rest on me. That is why, for Christ's sake, I delight in weaknesses, in insults, in hardships, in persecutions, in difficulties. For when I am weak, then I am strong."

Paul was given a thorn in his flesh to keep him from becoming proud because of the tremendous revelations God gave him. We are not told what Paul's "thorn" was. I think this is by design, so that every believer could identify their own weakness with Paul's. Paul takes his weakness to the Lord three times to plead with God to remove it.

But Paul is told that God allowed Satan to give him this thorn for his own good. Paul's great desire was to win people to Christ. The Lord tells him that he can do this better if he leaves the thorn because then, in his weakness, he would depend all the more on the Lord for strength. God's power is made complete in human weakness.

Therefore, Paul changes his prayer, "therefore I will boast all the more gladly about my weaknesses, so that Christ's power might rest on me … For when I am weak, then I am strong." God allowed the thorn to keep Paul from becoming proud. God would make it very obvious to Paul that Paul would be far more successful if he gets out of the way and allows God to work in him.

What is open theism? Does God change His mind?

Open theism teaches that God created mankind with total freedom over which God does not have total control. He is not omniscient (all-knowing) and cannot know perfectly how we will exercise our freedom. Nor can He know an event until it happens. Open theism holds that God changes or evolves with events, that He changes His mind or *repents*.

However, the Bible clearly teaches that God cannot change. He is the self-existent I AM (Exodus 3:14). He is perfect and never changes in His perfection (Malachi 3:6; Hebrews 1:12; James 1:17).

He is omniscient. He "knows the end from the beginning" (Isaiah 6:10). He is "infinite in understanding" (Psalm 147:5). He "foreknows" His elect (Romans 8:29; 2 Peter 1:2). And He does not change His mind (1 Samuel 15:29). When the Bible says "God repented" it is always in relation to mankind's repentance (Jonah 3). For instance, when God is ready to deal in judgment and the people repent or "change their mind" concerning their evil deeds, God then "changes His mind" and withholds his judgment. But ultimately God always knew that they would change their minds, so His "repenting" is only in His interactions with mankind.

If God cannot know an event until it happens, then He cannot know future events before they happen and all Bible prophesies that involve mankind's free acts are undermined.

Thus, open theism is not Biblical and constantly contradicts the Bible and robs God of many of His attributes.

Please explain "progressive revelation." I was told that it means the New Testament is more inspired than the Old Testament. Is this true?

No, absolutely not. The Bible is inspired in its totality, both the Old and the New Testament. Jesus constantly quoted the Old Testament as final authority. Progressive revelation means that more and more details were added to the revelation of God's redemption of mankind until Jesus Christ burst upon the scene. In contrast to this thinking and in truth, the New Testament was the perfect capstone built upon the perfect foundation of the Old Testament. The God of the Old Testament is revealed in His fullness in the person of Jesus Christ in the New Testament.

The Light of God's revelation started out as a flicker as it pointed to Him and grew brighter as the lamp was turned up until it grew to the brightness of the sun in its fullness. God chose Israel and set them apart that through them, "All the peoples of the earth will be blessed" (Genesis 12: 3).

It was through this nation that God's special revelation in Scripture was given. From this nation, God chose His penmen who would record His revelation to mankind – gradually, piece by piece, until the revelation was full and completed in Jesus Christ.

It was through His followers that the New Testament was completed as the capstone of God's revelation of redemption through Jesus Christ. "For the Law is only a shadow of the good things that are coming – not the realities themselves" (Hebrews 10:1).

The Old Testament law, the temple, the rituals, and the sacrifices were a shadow thrown against the wall of human history of the coming One as He approached and cast His shadow. The moral law and our inability to keep it show the necessity of His coming.

I am confused about faith and good works. My minister said God isn't interested in my good works. These would only offend a holy God. He's only concerned with my faith in his Son, Jesus Christ. So it does not matter how I live?

God is not interested in our good works refers to offering God good works to be saved. This is true. Salvation is not something that we can ever earn. Only God can provide salvation through faith in Christ. I do not know your minister, but it sounds to me like he is saying that God will not accept good works as far as salvation is concerned.

Christ purchased our salvation by taking our judgment on the cross. Of course, God would be offended if I ignored what Christ did on my behalf, thinking I could earn it by my good works. The Bible says I would be one who "trampled the Son of God under foot, who has treated as an unholy thing the blood of the covenant that sanctified him, and who has insulted the Spirit of grace" (Hebrew 10: 29).

Ephesians 2:8-9 says, "For it is by grace you have been saved, through faith – and this not from yourselves, it is the gift of God – not by works, so that no one can boast." So we see that we are not saved by good works. However, the next verse says, "For we are God's workmanship, created in Christ Jesus to do good works, which God prepared in advance for us to do" (Ephesians 2:10).

Here we see that while we are not saved by works, we are saved to do good works. So we see that while God wants us to do good works, and expects us to do good works, it is not to earn salvation (this is legalism) but because we have been saved freely by faith. The Holy Spirit enters us and motivates us to do good works because we have been saved. God does accept good works from us out of gratitude, and He will even reward us for them but never as a payment for anything we have done.

Romans 10: 4 says, "Christ is the end of the law so that there may be righteousness for everyone who believes."

Here the Greek word for *end* is *telos* and has the two combined thoughts of *goal* and *fulfillment*. This means that Christ was the *goal* to which the law was aimed when it presented God's holy demands that men could not obey because of their sinfulness. Christ was the goal of the law. The sacrifices pointed to Christ and His sacrifice for sin. He was the fulfillment of the law. His death on the cross fulfilled and ended the whole Levitical system, which was signified by the rending of the veil in the temple.

Isn't it narrow-minded to say that Jesus is the only way to God?

Clearly, Jesus claimed to be the only way to God. In John 14:6-7 Jesus said, "I am the way and the truth and the life. No one comes to the Father except through me. If you really knew me, you would know my Father as well. From now on you know Him and have seen Him." Jesus is the only way to God the Father because He is one with the Father. Jesus came from the Father, in union with the Father, to bring us to the Father.

All truth is narrow. Two plus two equals four, no more and no less. Jesus does not leave room to be broad-minded on this subject. The way to God is narrow, the truth of God is narrow, and the way to eternal life is narrow.

In Matthew 7:13-14 Jesus warned, "Enter through the narrow gate. For wide is the gate and broad is the road that leads to destruction, and many enter through it. But small is the gate and narrow the road that leads to life, and only a few find it."

By the coming of Jesus Christ, the world is confronted with a crisis: "For God so loved the world that He gave his one and only Son, that whoever believes in Him shall not perish but have eternal life. For God did not send His Son into the world to condemn the world, but to save the world through Him. Whoever believes in Him is not condemned, but whoever does not believe stands condemned already because he does not believe in the name of God's one and only Son" (John 3:16-18).

Only Jesus provides us a way to God through His death and resurrection. Only this deals with the problem of man's sin. The whole subject is summed up in Acts 4:12: "Salvation is found in no one else, for there is no other name under heaven given to men by which we must be saved."

What is the unforgivable sin? Can Christians commit it?

The unforgivable sin is not a single sin but an attitude of determined unbelief.

When the Holy Spirit brings a person to conviction of his or her need of Christ and they continue to resist in determined rejection, the Holy Spirit ceases convicting that person because that person chooses to hold on to their sins, and He gives them over to their sins. John 3:19 refers to this: "This is the verdict: light has come into the world, but men loved darkness instead of light because their deeds were evil."

This is brought out in Romans 1:28: "Furthermore, since they did not think it worthwhile to retain the knowledge of God, He gave them over to a depraved mind, to do what ought not to be done."

God turns them over to their own ways as hopelessly unwilling to come to Him. We see this in Matthew 23:37-38 where Jesus wept over Jerusalem: "How often I have longed to gather your children together, as a hen gathers her chicks under her wings, but you were not willing. Look, your house is left to you desolate."

They had rejected all His invitations. He was willing but they were set in their stubborn unbelief. He was about to leave and He tells them that the temple that was the house of God is no longer God's house but "your house." They had rejected the God of the temple, and He was leaving.

Once the heart is hardened to the point of a determined, set resistance against the Holy Spirit's conviction, God turns them over to their choice. We are warned in Hebrews 3:8, "So, as the Holy Spirit says: 'Today, if you hear His voice, do not harden your hearts.'"

And in Hebrews 3:12-13 we are again warned, "See to it, brothers, that none of you has a sinful, unbelieving heart that turns away from the living God. But encourage one another daily, as long as it is called today, so that none of you may be hardened by sin's deceitfulness." In Hosea 4:17 we read the sad words, "Ephraim is joined to idols; leave him alone!" Ephraim was "joined" – set in his ways to hold on to his idols, so God turns him over to them.

Hebrew 6:4-6 again warns, "It is impossible for those who have once been enlightened, who have tasted the heavenly gift, who have shared in the Holy Spirit, who have tasted the goodness of the word of God and the powers of the coming age, if they fall away, to be brought back to repentance."

Here we are told that those who have been led by the Holy Spirit to see their need of Christ and then fall away from this conviction by hardening their hearts to the Spirit's pleading (rejecting the conviction that God was good enough to give them) will have hardened their hearts so that they cannot respond to the Spirit's drawing them.

Obviously, a true Christian, (by which I mean a person who is born-again rather than a person who merely calls himself a Christian) cannot commit this sin since he or she has already trusted in Christ and belongs to God.

Do Paul and James contradict each other? Are we saved by faith or by works? (James 2:14-26; Romans 3:28.)

In Romans 3:28 Paul writes, "We maintain that a man is justified by faith apart from observing the law." James is not contradicting salvation by faith. But it is not a dead faith but a living faith that motivates our actions. James is simply defining true, saving faith. "What good is it, my brothers, if a man claims to have faith but has no deeds? Can such faith save him?"

James infers that if that kind of faith can save him, it is a dead faith, lifeless. It produces no works. "Show me your faith without deeds, and I will show you my faith by what I do. You believe that there is one God. Good! Even the demons believe that – and shudder." A person can believe the historical facts about Jesus (this is important), but a mere mental acknowledgment is not enough. Even demons believe in that sense, but True Faith must change our lives.

Verses 21-24 show that Abraham had a true living faith, one that was active and not dormant. In verses 25-26, we see that the prostitute Rahab showed her living faith by protecting the spies sent by Joshua (Joshua Chapter 2). So clearly there is no contradiction between Paul and James.

How can man have free will when everything is foreknown and foreordained by God. Acts 13:48 says: "When the Gentiles heard this, they were glad and honored the word of the Lord; and all who were appointed for eternal life believed." Please explain.

We must understand what foreknowledge and foreordination means. It does not mean that mankind is not free in their choices. Mankind's actions are not based on God's foreknowledge. Rather God's foreknowledge is based on what mankind will freely do. Foreknowledge is based on fact; fact is not based on foreknowledge.

The word *foreordained* means *chosen by God*. I Peter 1:20 in the King James Version Bible says that Christ was "foreordained" before the creation of the world to die for our sins. The New International Version Bible says the Christ was "chosen" by God to be the sacrifice for the sins of the world.

This means that God did not cause Judas to betray Christ but that God included Judas' and the Sanhedrin's free will into His plan. God knew from eternity what each person would do with their free will, and God made plans based on their acceptance of the Lord Jesus Christ. They were ordained (appointed to eternal life) based on His foreknowledge.

All those who will receive Christ are ordained to eternal life. If any are lost, it is because they refuse to come to Christ and receive the free gift of eternal life: "You diligently study the Scriptures because you think that by them you possess eternal life. These are the Scriptures that testify about me. Yet you refuse to come to me to have life" (John 5:40). "He is patient with you, not wanting anyone to perish, but everyone to come to repentance" (2 Peter 3:8).

In Revelation 22:17 John is about to close the last Book of the Bible. The Holy Spirit moves him to end with a final invitation: "The Spirit and the bride say, 'Come!' And let him who hears say, 'Come!' Whoever is thirsty, let him come; and whoever wishes, let him take the free gift of the water of life."

Does the book of Hebrews teach that a Christian can apostatize?

The "falling away" recorded in the Book of Hebrews 5:11 to 6:6 refers to first century Jews who had been led by the Holy Spirit to leave Judaism and confess Christ and then were in danger of resisting the Holy Spirit under pressure of persecution, hardening their hearts against the conviction of the Holy Spirit. These people went back to the *elementary* or beginning and incomplete teachings about Christ under the Old Testament system of types and foreshadows.

They are warned in Hebrews 3:7-8, "So as the Holy Spirit says: 'Today, if you hear His voice, do not harden your hearts.'" They were led by the Holy Spirit to see their need of Christ, but after repeated resistance they were in danger of grieving the Spirit away: "If we deliberately keep on sinning [by hardening our hearts] after we have received the knowledge of the truth [after the Holy Spirit convicts us of our need of Christ], no sacrifice for sin is left [if Christ is rejected, there is no other sacrifice for sin], but only a fearful expectation of judgment and a raging fire that will consume the enemies of God" (Hebrews 10:26-27).

In Hebrews 10:29 these people are said to have "trampled the Son of God under foot, who has treated as an unholy thing the blood of the covenant that sanctified him, and who has insulted the Spirit of Grace?"

To harden our hearts to the Holy Spirit's conviction of our need of Christ is to walk on the blood of Christ as a common thing, which insults the Holy Spirit who has brought this conviction to us.

Christians who are truly born again cannot lose their salvation because the Holy Spirit lives in them. But unbelievers who are on the verge of receiving Christ can harden their hearts to the Holy Spirit's conviction and "fall away" from receiving Christ.

Why do the genealogies in Matthew and Luke differ?

Matthew gives the genealogy of Joseph and Luke records Mary's genealogy. Jesus was the legal son of Joseph through adoption. Matthew 1:16 reads, "and Jacob the father of Joseph, the husband of Mary, of whom was born Jesus, who is called the Christ." The Scripture is very careful to show that Jesus was not the physical son of Joseph. The words *of whom* in the original Greek are feminine and refer to Mary.

Luke, who records Mary's genealogy in 1:32-33 reads, "He will be great and will be called the Son of the Most High. The Lord will give Him the throne of his father David, and He shall reign over the house of Jacob forever, his kingdom will never end." Joseph was descended from David through Solomon (Matthew 1:6) and Jesus was the legal son of Joseph by adoption. The kingship passed through the male line, while Mary was descended through Nathan, another son of David (Luke 3:31). Jesus was the descendant of David through Mary.

Can you explain God's sovereignty and man's free will?

Many people believe that God cannot be sovereign unless He makes every decision that is made and that everything is done only as He causes it, including who will receive Christ and who will reject Him. With this line of thinking, there is no human free will, and all of man's sin is because God, in His sovereignty, has ordained that these sins be committed, after which He holds these people whom He caused to sin to be held accountable for these sins that he caused them to commit! And these same people who hold this view will tell you that it is a great mystery how God's will moves everything, including all man's decisions, and yet man is accountable for the decisions that God makes for him!

However, this is not the teaching of Scripture. The Scriptures clearly teach that God gave man free will in the Garden of Eden to choose or reject His authority over them. Adam and Eve, and thus all mankind, chose to reject God's authority over them. In God's infinite love and sovereignty, He sent Christ to redeem mankind and gave them the choice of receiving or rejecting Christ.

But based on His foreknowledge, God *chose* or *elected* those He knew would believe and did not have to wait until mankind's actual decision. Thus, He predestinated those who would receive Christ and wrote their names in His Book of Life before they were born.

God Himself tells us that if He simply, sovereignly elected men and women, He would have elected everyone as 1 Timothy 2:4-6 informs: "God wants all men to be saved and to come to the knowledge of the truth. For there is one God, and one Mediator between God and men, the man Christ Jesus, who gave Himself as a ransom for all men."

This passage says it all concerning election and God's sovereignty. God wanted all mankind to be saved and come to the knowledge of the truth. This passage goes on to explain what God did because He wanted all men to be saved. He sent Christ to give himself as a ransom for all men. This tells us that God's love is not limited nor was Christ's atonement for sin limited but was a ransom for all mankind. It is important to make it clear here that in many places when Scripture refers to *man* in a universal sense, it is the generic form of *mankind*.

God's love and Christ's redemptive work were for all mankind. They were not only for all *kinds* of people but for each individual of the *kinds* of people. The crucifixion of Jesus Christ was God embracing the whole world with the bloody hands of the Redeemer.

There truly is no real mystery of how God can be sovereign and mankind have free will. God's sovereignty simply takes into consideration mankind's free will.

Where was Jesus for three days between His death and resurrection?

The dying thief on the cross next to Jesus said, "'Jesus, remember me when you come into your kingdom.' Jesus answered him, 'I tell you the truth, today you will be with me in paradise.'" Paul uses the term "paradise" in 2 Corinthians 12:4 and identifies it with the third heaven. Jesus refers to it as "the Father's house" (John 14:2). Jesus' body was placed in the tomb while His human spirit went to heaven with the thief who put his faith in Christ.

Some teach that Jesus went to hell and battled Satan and completed our salvation there. But the hell that Jesus suffered was on the cross where He was judged for our sins. It was while He was on the cross that Jesus cried out, "It is finished," and bowed His head and died. In the Greek, it is one word, *tetelestia*, a word used in connection with a debt being paid and means that the debt is *finished* or *paid in full*. The debt is *ended* or *completed*, *fulfilled* or *finished*. And it is done so *forever* or *once for all* Satan was completely defeated on the Cross for all those who put their faith in Christ.

What is the difference between mercy and grace?

Mercy means forgiveness, or not getting what we deserve, but the Biblical use of "grace" means much more. It means receiving the opposite of what we deserve. On the cross, God dealt with Jesus as though He was the sinner, the opposite of what He deserved. When the sinner comes to Christ, God deals with him as though he were His Son, the opposite of what we deserve. Jesus took our sins and God gave us Christ's righteousness. This amazing exchange is called *Grace*.

This is what it means to be in Christ. "Therefore, if anyone is in Christ, he is a new creation; the old has gone, the new has come" (2 Corinthian 5:17). Believers in Christ have entered into a whole new relationship to God and have entered into all the benefits of Christ's death and resurrection. God now sees them as being in Christ, sharing in Christ's relationship with God. They have become totally new creations. Their position and all their relationships to Adam and his fallen race under condemnation are forever passed away, and they now have a new position and relationship to God and the new creation.

Ephesians 2:4-7 says it all: "But because of his great love for us, God, who is rich in mercy, made us alive with Christ even when we were dead in transgressions – it is by grace you have been saved. And God raised us up with Christ and seated us with Him in the heavenly realms in Christ Jesus, in order that in the coming ages He might show the incomparable riches of His grace, expressed in His kindness to us in Christ Jesus."

What is the significance of baptism?

Water baptism is the outward testimony or sign of an inward reality of being born again. It means the entry into fellowship with believers through Christ's death and resurrection, symbolized by going under the water and rising out of it. It symbolizes that our old way of living is buried and we now live by Christ's resurrection life. Obviously, it is only for true believers; otherwise the symbolism has no real meaning.

This outward baptism with water symbolizes the inward washing away of our sins through faith in Christ: "He saved us through the washing of rebirth and renewal by the Holy Spirit" (Titus 3:5). Through faith in Christ, the Holy Spirit washes away our sins and imparts the new birth. Jesus referred to this as being "born of the water and the spirit" (John 3:5). It is not some magical ritual that gives us a relationship with God. It does not impart anything to the recipients. It is a symbol of faith in Jesus Christ that does impart the new birth and the washing away of our sins.

How can there be only one faith? Isn't it arrogant to try to convert others to your Christian religion? Are not all the other religions equally good and meet the needs of their followers?

I take it that you mean "How can there be only one true faith?" Well, they can't all be true when they contradict each other; the choice must be narrowed down by each person. I do not think it is arrogant to try to convert others to the Christian religion, but it is narrow.

In Matthew 7:13-14 Jesus says concerning the way to heaven, "Enter through the narrow gate. For wide is the gate and broad the road that leads to destruction, and many enter through it. But small is the gate and narrow the road that leads to life, and only a few find it."

All truth is narrow. Two plus two always equals four, no more and no less, exactly four. In John 14:6 Jesus said, "I am the way and the truth and the life. No one comes to the Father except through me." Here Jesus states it very clearly. If Jesus was wrong, then he is a false prophet and is not a way to the Father. But if He is right, then He is the only way. Jesus does not play our game of political correctness.

In John 10:7-9 Jesus said, "I tell you the truth, I am the gate for the sheep. All who came before me were thieves and robbers, but the sheep did not listen to them. I am the gate; whoever enters through me will be saved." Here again Jesus is to the point. He does not beat around the bush. This question is too serious.

John 3:16-18 is very plain and simple: "For God so loved the world that He gave His one and only Son, that whoever believes in him shall not perish but have eternal life. For God did not send His Son into the world to condemn the world, but to save the world through him. Whoever believes in him is not condemned, but whoever does not believe stands condemned already because he has not believed in the name of God's one and only Son."

Jesus tells us as clearly and simply as words can convey that we are not to put Him in a group of many saviors. He stands unique and alone. This has confronted Christianity from the beginning with torture racks and death. The Roman Empire allowed the worship of many gods so long as they acknowledged that Caesar was Lord.

But the early Christians refused to acknowledge any but Jesus alone, as Jesus demanded. The narrow road to eternal life is the road of Jesus, and the wide road to destruction is as wide as all the other religions.

How can we forgive someone who has really hurt us?

The answer is given in Philippians 4:13: "I can do everything through Him who strengthens me." I remember years ago I was confronted with this problem, as all Christians are. I knew God was telling me to forgive someone, and I did not think it was possible for me to do so. I felt trapped because I knew God wanted me to forgive him, but at the same time I knew He did not want me to simply go through the motions but to honestly forgive him with heart-felt sincerity.

While I was in the process of telling Him how hard it was for me to truly forgive him, I could hear Jesus say, "Can you do it for me?" That made all the difference in the world and God gave me insight into Philippians 4:13. Not only could I forgive him for Jesus, I found joy and peace and healing. I felt privileged and honored that I could do something hard for Jesus. It was a sense of total freedom. What was impossible for me to do, I could do for Jesus. Many times since then I have been confronted with this same problem, and each time I found that I can do all things through Christ.

How can a Christian live a life of blessing from God? So much of the Christian life seems to be hardship rather than blessing. Can you explain this?

I cannot explain anything by my own wisdom, but thank God He has given us a revelation of all the mysteries of life and the Author of this revelation is with His people to enable them to grasp those mysteries.

First of all, in love God demands that we abandon our lives to Him through Christ forever, "I urge you, brothers, in view of God's mercy to offer your bodies as living sacrifices, holy and pleasing to God – this is your spiritual act of worship."

We were created to be managed by God. God never intended that his people should stand on their own. The very core of sin is independence of God. This is our great problem. We want to do it all ourselves. Any Christian who wants God's blessing on his life must meet His conditions. But because, though redeemed, we are still sinners and constantly want to second-guess God, this is not easy to do. But God will enable us if we will simply trust Him through every obstacle. We must make up our minds to give ourselves to God and to be used as His servants forever. This is crucial because this is what we lost in the fall. God has the right to set the terms, as He insists on being in charge. He allowed us to be in charge at one time, and we made a disaster of it.

The first demand of God is trust in His purpose for us. He must set the agenda, not us. No loving father would allow the child to be in charge of his own life, no matter how much he demands it. We are dealing with the Living God, and He will not let us bargain with Him. Not because He's stubborn and selfish, but because only He is capable of working things out. His demands are always wise and loving.

We must insist with God that Christ has the right to first place in our hearts and lives: "Do you not know that your body is a temple of the Holy Spirit, who is in you, whom you have received from God? You are not your own; you were bought at a price. Therefore honor God with your body" (1 Corinthians 6:19-20). We must choose to follow God's way to receive God's blessing.

We must realize that many hardships and trials in our Christian lives are really blessings in disguise to lead us to trust and depend on God and draw closer to Him.

Jesus said, "Anyone who does not carry his cross and follow me cannot be my disciple" (Luke 14:27).

He was not referring to our physical infirmities, weaknesses, and troubles. These are unavoidable and the common lot of all humanity, whether Christian or non-Christian. His disciples knew what it meant to carry one's cross from watching the victims of crucifixion carrying their crosses to the execution site. It is a sharing, in one sense, of Christ's cross. It meant death for Him and it will mean death for us – death to ourselves.

Christ's cross was what He was willing to endure that the will of the Father might be fulfilled. The believer's cross is what he must face as He seeks to fulfill the will of God. It is our identifying with Christ. It is telling God, "not my will, but yours be done." It is to have all our ambitions and desires put to death so that we can fulfill His will for our lives.

Jesus said, "You call me 'Teacher and Lord,' and rightly so, for that is what I am" (John 13:13). Total commitment to Christ is at the heart of Christian experience and service. In Philippians 3:8 Paul said, "What is more, I consider everything as loss compared to the surpassing greatness of knowing Christ Jesus my Lord, for whose sake I have lost all things. I consider them rubbish, that I may gain Christ."

"Since, then, you have been raised with Christ, set your hearts on things above, where Christ is seated at the right hand of God. Set your minds on things above, not on earthly things. For you died, and your life is now hidden with Christ in God. When Christ, who is your life, appears, then you also will appear with Him in glory" (Colossians 3: 1-4).

5. Constantine

Was Constantine a Christian?

This is hard to figure out. On the one hand, it would not make sense for him to come out in favor of Christianity to gain the support of Christians. When he did this, his main supporters were pagans who despised the Christians. Christians made up a small minority and mostly belonged to the poor lower classes with little to contribute to his cause. This seems to favor his conversion being genuine.

While on the other hand, his *conversion* did not stop him from believing in other gods. Throughout his career he seems to have thought that the Unconquered Sun god and the Christian God were the same; that is, two views of the same God. The other gods were still real and powerful to him, and he would at times consult the oracle of Apollo. He accepted the title of High Priest of paganism and led in all kinds of pagan ceremonies, with no concern that he was betraying the God who had given him victory.

The evidence seems to say that Constantine was a *Christian* outwardly, but not inwardly. In other words, he went along with the outward trappings of Christianity but not the inward reality.

What part did Constantine have in Christianity? Didn't he have Christians murdered?

Constantine legalized Christianity and made it the favored, though not yet official, religion of the Empire. When Constantine was fighting for mastery of the Roman Empire, he gathered his army in Gaul and crossed the Alps and returned to Italy and moved onto Rome, the capital of his enemy Maxentius. The two armies met at the battle of the Milvian Bridge in 312. On the eve of the battle, Constantine said he saw a vision in the sky of a cross, with the words, "in this you shall conquer." Then that night he had a dream in which he was commanded to place a Christian symbol on his soldiers' shields and standards.

The battle was won by Constantine, and Maxentius fell into the river and drowned. Then Constantine became the lone master of the entire western half of the Roman Empire. After further battles with Licinius, Constantine emerged as the supreme ruler of the entire Roman Empire.

Out of this relationship between the church and the emperor grew the church and state entanglement of the later Roman Empire. Constantine kept the title of the pagan high priest, Pontifex Maximus; his coins still featured some of the pagan gods, notably the Unconquered Sun, from his previous religion. These were maintained for a decade after his *conversion*.

The Roman church adopted many pagan beliefs and images. December 25 was the birthday of the Sun; Saturnalia, the Roman winter festival of December 17-23, celebrated the festivities of the giving of gifts and candles and incense of later Christmases.

Many other pagan symbols were Christianized. Several associated Mary with Isis, the Egyptian goddess whose worship had spread throughout the Empire. Isis became identified with many other goddesses of other nations and was the universal mother of later pagan religions.

Isis was called the *Great Virgin* and *Mother of the God* and was naturally identified with Mary. Some surviving images of Isis holding the child Horus are in a pose remarkably like some of the early Christian Madonnas.

In many places, saints took the place of pagan gods. While the church never went so far as to say that saints were to be worshipped, it was said that they were in a favored position of influence to hear prayer and present them directly to God. Eventually, relics were said to have miraculous powers. Constantine's mother, Empress Helena, gave momentum to this when on a pilgrimage to the Holy Land she claimed to have discovered the very cross on which Christ was crucified. Soon the cross was said to have miraculous powers, and pieces of wood from it were found all over the Roman Empire.

Until Constantine, Christian worship had been simple and humble. At first they worshipped in private homes. After Constantine's conversion, Christian worship began to be influenced by imperial splendor. Ministers who had worn everyday clothes began to dress in luxurious garments. Churches built in the time of Constantine were kingly palaces. Instead of simple preaching by a pastor, the church took the form of a hierarchy of priests, bishops and archbishops, etc.

The day of worship was the "first day of the week," the day of Christ's resurrection and is distinct from the Jewish Sabbath under the Law, according to the gospels, which was a "day of rest." But under Constantine, Sunday was recognized as the "Sabbath" and was decreed as "a day of rest" in A.D. 321. Jews were legally discriminated against as evil haters of good.

The Da Vinci code says that Emperor Constantine stopped goddess worship, changed the day of worship from Saturday to Sunday, made Jesus divine, and established the biblical canon at the council of Nicaea in the early fourth century.

But the council of Nicaea did none of these. Goddess worship was never a part of the early church. Sunday – "the first day of the week" – was recognized as the day of worship from the time of Jesus' resurrection. The deity of Christ had been affirmed for almost three hundred years by the time of Nicaea on May 20, 325. Jesus was worshipped and confessed as universal Lord. This was the stance of the Church from the beginning, as we can see from the writings of Paul, the four gospels, and other New Testament writings.

The Biblical canon had already been established. By the second century, the church leaders had already quoted the four gospels and only them, thousands of times in their writings; the present New Testament was cited more the 36,000 times.

Sunday was the established day of worship from the very beginning. The resurrection of Jesus Christ was the beginning of a new dispensation, from the law to grace. The Sabbath was never changed but rather it was fulfilled and done away with by Christ.

6. George Washington

Was George Washington a Deist? I have read a few authors who said he was a Deist and did not believe in a personal God but referred to Him as "Providence." What is the truth about his faith?

We must first understand what deists believe. They believe what Einstein believed – a belief in an impersonal God who created the universe and set it in motion and then abandoned it to run on its own. He abandoned all control over it or any influence on the affairs of humanity.

Washington's use of providence meant the opposite. Providence refers to God's governing and controlling all things within certain bounds, overruling and directing according to His eternal purpose. This includes man's free will. He does not interfere with free will, but He does direct it. This includes man's good and sinful actions. Sinful actions are allowed and never caused or approved of by Him but controlled and directed by Him for good. God's controlling evil for good is vividly illustrated in the life of Joseph, whose brothers hated him, faked his death to their father Jacob, and sold him into slavery. Then he was falsely accused of a crime against his master's wife and thrown into prison.

But God overruled and controlled their sinful actions and while in prison he interpreted some dreams that led him to be placed in charge of Egypt's food supply during a great famine. He was made ruler under pharaoh and saved many lives including his own family. At every turn,

God had overruled evil intensions for good. When the famine hit Israel and affected his family, his father sent his sons to Egypt to buy food, and they were put at Joseph's mercy.

His brothers were afraid when they faced Joseph and threw themselves before him and said, "We are your slaves." Joseph then explained about God's overruling providence, "You intended to harm me, but God intended it for good to accomplish what is now being done, the saving of many lives. So then, don't be afraid, I will provide for you and your children."

George Washington appealing to providence is the opposite of what a deist would do. He was known for beseeching God in prayer and for his giving thanks for God's help and blessing as a personal God, who was vitally concerned about His creation. On March 11, 1792, President Washington wrote a letter to John Armstrong from Philadelphia: "I am sure that never was a people, who had more reason to acknowledge a Divine interposition in their affairs, than those of the United States; and I should be pained to believe that they have forgotten that, which was so often manifested during our Revolution, or that they failed to consider the omnipotence of that God who is alone able to protect them."

As he neared death, he asked everyone to leave his room so he could spend time alone with God. Later he said to his secretary, Tobias Lear, "Tis well." Then he folded his hands and folded his arm across his chest, closed his eyes, and said, "Father of mercies, take me to Thyself."

As President, he many times called for days of prayer and thanksgiving for God's protection and care of America. As commander of the American army and as president of the United States, he took time to spend two hours in the Bible and prayer. George Washington was a true Christian and by the true standard of greatness he was one of the greatest men that America ever produced.

7. Abraham Lincoln

It is my understanding that Abraham Lincoln was not a believer in Christ. Is this true?

At first Lincoln, who suffered from depression and had a pretty rough life, was not a believer in Christ. His mother died when he was nine years old. Shortly after that, his sister died. When he went to Springfield, he befriended some skeptical friends who gave him a volume attacking the Bible, causing him to become very skeptical, and openly said that he was not a believer in Christ. However, he was a believer in an overruling power rather than in a personal God. He would even scoff at the Bible and ridicule it.

One day, he saw slaves being sold and families being broken up and sold to different buyers. He vowed that if God ever gave him a position that would enable him to do something about slavery, he would do it.

In 1857, the Supreme Court in the Dred Scott case decided that slaves were not persons or citizens but were the property of their owner, the same as for their horses and cattle, and the owner had the freedom to do what they wanted with their own property. In his inaugural address on March 4, 1861, Lincoln expressed his disagreement with the court.

On September 22, 1862, after the massive Confederate army was defeated at the Battle Antietam by Union troops, Lincoln spoke to his cabinet and said, "I made a vow to Almighty God that if He would grant victory to our army in Antietam and General Lee driven back from Maryland, that I would emancipate the slaves." Three days later, Lincoln went public with the preliminary Emancipation Proclamation, which he signed into law on January 1, 1863.

Lincoln was becoming more and more aware of God's hand in the affairs of men. In December 1862 he said, "The ways of God are mysterious and profound beyond all comprehension – who by searching can find Him out. God only knows the issue of this business. He has destroyed nations from the map of history for their sins. Nevertheless, my hopes prevail generally above my fears for the republic. The times are dark, the spirits of ruin are abroad in all their power, and the mercy of God alone can save us."

When his beloved little boy of 12 died, Lincoln was overwhelmed with grief. Dr. Vinton came to visit and told the president that it was not right to mourn over his son like this: "Your son is alive in Paradise with Christ." Lincoln was dumfounded and said, "Alive! Alive! Surely you mock me." Vinton assured him that it was true. Lincoln jumped up and threw his arms around the pastor, sobbing, "Alive! Alive! My boy is alive!"

An Illinois clergyman who talked to Lincoln after that said, "Mr. President, do you love Jesus?" After a long pause, the president solemnly replied, "When I left Springfield, I asked the people to pray for me, but I was not a Christian. When I buried my son, the severest trial of my life, I was not Christian. But when I went to Gettysburg and saw the graves of thousands of our soldiers, I then and there consecrated myself to Christ. Yes, I do love Jesus."

After that, he spent much more time reading the Bible, praying, and attending church on Sundays and Wednesdays until his assassination three years later.

Lincoln's pastor, Dr. Phineas Gurley of the New York Avenue Presbyterian Church, said, "The death of Willie Lincoln in 1862 and the visit to Gettysburg battlefield in 1863 finally led Lincoln to personal faith in Christ." Dr. Gurley said Lincoln wanted to make a public profession of his faith in Christ on Easter Sunday morning, but he was assassinated on Good Friday at Ford's Theater by John Wilkes Booth.

The last act of Congress signed into law by Lincoln was that the motto *In God we trust* should be inscribed on our coins. It is no coincidence that Lincoln's hero was George Washington. He carried his biography and read it often. And like Washington, Lincoln became one of the greatest men that America, or even the world, ever produced.

www.ingramcontent.com/pod-product-compliance
Lightning Source LLC
Chambersburg PA
CBHW050436010526
44118CB00013B/1549